Struggle and
Suffrage in Plymouth

Struggle and Suffrage in Plymouth:

Women's Lives and the Fight for Equality

Tracey Glasspool

PEN & SWORD HISTORY

AN IMPRINT OF PEN & SWORD BOOKS LTD.
YORKSHIRE - PHILADELPHIA

First published in Great Britain in 2019 by
Pen & Sword HISTORY
An imprint of
Pen & Sword Books Ltd
Yorkshire – Philadelphia

ISBN 978 1 52671 676 7

A CIP catalogue record for this book is
available from the British Library.

Printed and bound in England by CPI Group (UK) Ltd, Croydon, CR0 4YY

Pen & Sword Books Limited incorporates the imprints of Atlas, Archaeology,
Aviation, Discovery, Family History, Fiction, History, Maritime, Military,
Military Classics, Politics, Select, Transport, True Crime, Air World, Frontline
Publishing, Leo Cooper, Remember When, Seaforth Publishing, The Praetorian
Press, Wharncliffe Local History, Wharncliffe Transport, Wharncliffe True
Crime and White Owl.

For a complete list of Pen & Sword titles please contact
PEN & SWORD BOOKS LIMITED
47 Church Street, Barnsley, South Yorkshire, S70 2AS, England
E-mail: enquiries@pen-and-sword.co.uk
Website: www.pen-and-sword.co.uk

Or

PEN AND SWORD BOOKS
1950 Lawrence Rd, Havertown, PA 19083, USA
E-mail: Uspen-and-sword@casematepublishers.com
Website: www.penandswordbooks.com

Contents

Acknowledgements

Thank you to the following people and organisations:

Clare Robinson of the South West Image Bank, Paul Santillo and Peter McCarthy of Devon Naval Heritage Centre, Plymouth Central Library, Plymouth and West Devon Record Office, Aggies.org.uk, Edinburgh University, The Western Morning News. And last, but not least, to the four Glasspool boys, for their unique brand of support.

Abbreviations Used

ASL: Anti-Suffrage League
ATS: Auxiliary Territorial Service
LNA: Ladies National Association for Repeal of the Contagious Diseases Acts
NUWSS: National Union of Women's Suffrage Societies
PCA: Plymouth Citizens' Association
PWDRO: Plymouth and West Devon Record Office
QAIMNS: Queen Alexandra's Imperial Military Nursing Service
TANS: Territorial Army Nursing Service
VAD: Voluntary Aid Detachments
WAAC: Women's Army Auxiliary Corps
WDM: Western Daily Mercury
WMN: Western Morning News
WRNS: Women's Royal Naval Service
WSPU: Women's Social and Political Union
WVS: Women's Voluntary Service

CHAPTER 1

The Changing Role of Women

'Plymouth is a town of women...'

Women's Lives 1850–1950

The period from 1850 to 1950 was a time of transformation in the lives of women. A woman of the 1850s had no vote, limited opportunities in education and employment, could not graduate from university or enter the professions. On marriage her wealth and property passed to her husband and she had no legal identity of her own. Her role was that of home-maker, wife and mother.

One hundred years later, a woman could both vote in and stand for municipal and parliamentary elections. Her education was better and her employment opportunities far wider. She could graduate from university, and the professions were now open to her. She retained control of her own property and earnings on marriage, her family was smaller and her health better. Although the domestic role continued to dominate and there were many reforms still to come, women were on course for equality with men.

But this transformation did not come without struggle and the residents of Plymouth were not found wanting in the fight for women's rights. From Nancy Astor, the first female MP to take her seat in Parliament, to Mabel Ramsay, dedicated doctor and suffrage supporter; from pioneering birth control clinics to campaigns for women police to lady footballers – Plymouth was not afraid to take a stance.

By the mid-nineteenth century, increasing industrialisation had caused a proliferation of factories, mills and workshops. When work had taken place in small family workshops or at home women played an integral part, but now they became disconnected from the workplace and the concept of separate male and female spheres emerged. The male sphere was the public and political one; men were the employers and the employed, the breadwinners, the politicians and the lawmakers, debating and creating the rules by which society lived. By contrast the female sphere was the private one – that of the home and family. For the middle classes, a woman was seen as the 'angel in the house', raising and nurturing children and running a perfect home. For working-class women life was more complicated. Both single and married women needed to work but options were restricted and poorly paid. Housing was often little more than slums, families were large and health poor.

The concept of separate spheres and the domestic, nurturing, child-bearing role of women permeated all aspects of their lives, defining and limiting their opportunities. There was much debate about what women were capable of, and what they needed to be protected from, to ensure this role was not compromised. Gradually however, there began a chafing at these restrictions, thanks to committed women such as those involved in London's Langham Place Group and the Kensington Society, as well as women in towns and cities all over the country, Plymouth included. Women with time, resources and resourcefulness began to debate the inequalities they faced and to petition and protest for change. The result was a burgeoning feminist movement with campaigns for women's suffrage, access to higher education, better employment opportunities and women's rights in marriage.

This book aims to provide an accessible introduction to the reforms which took place over the period, the consequences for society and the place of women within it, with a focus on the women of, and events in, Plymouth. It will consider changes to employment and education laws, the impact of the two world wars, the suffrage campaign and political world, along with health, housing and maternity issues. Figure 1.1 highlights some of the major events of the period and the Acts of Parliament which will be considered in more detail.

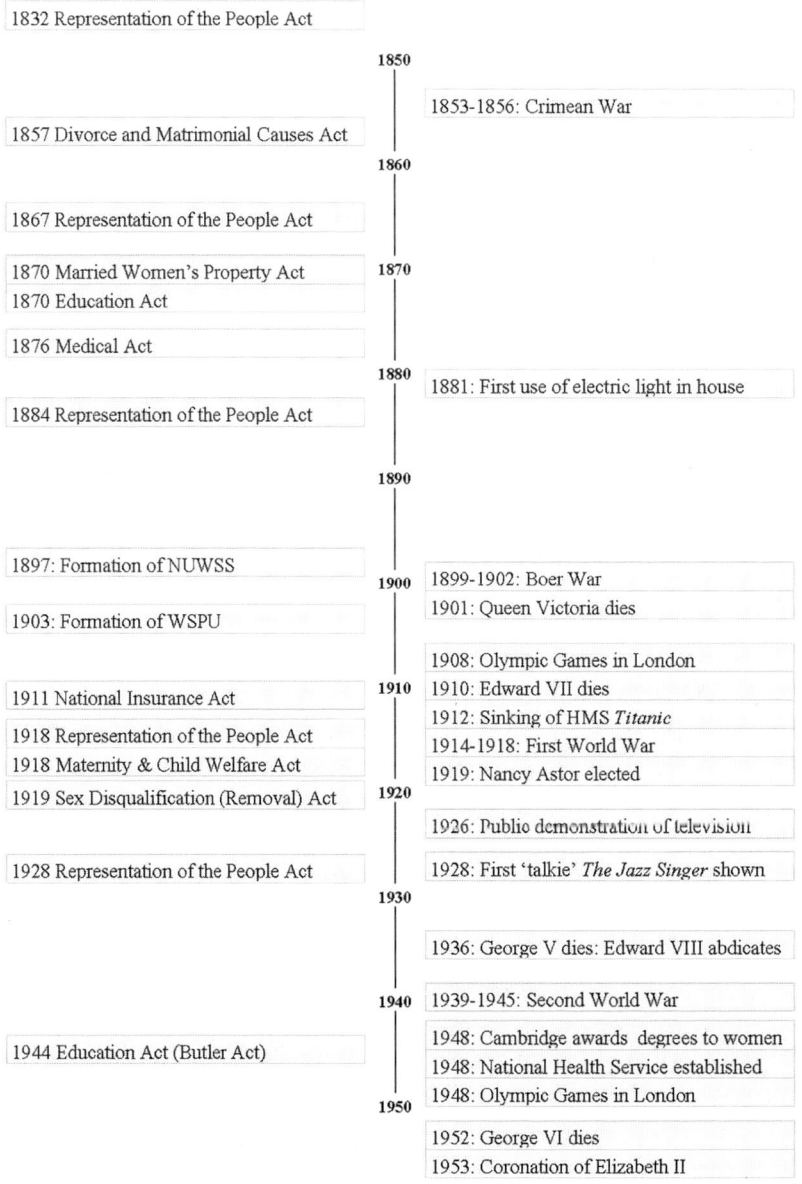

Fig. 1.1: Timeline c1850-1950

A Brief History of Plymouth

How women lived is interwoven with the character of *where* they lived and as this book is concerned with the women of Plymouth, it is worth spending a moment to consider the nature and history of this maritime city. Today's Plymouth was originally made up of the Three Towns of Plymouth, Devonport and East Stonehouse which were joined as one borough in 1914. City status was granted in October 1928. Plymouth's coastal location and its strategic importance in both trade and defence shaped its history and character. Many famous names set sail from its ports, including Sir Walter Raleigh, Richard Hawkins, and Sir Francis Drake, Vice-Admiral of the fleet which overcame the Spanish Armada in 1588. In 1620 the Pilgrim Fathers set sail in the Mayflower from Plymouth to Massachusetts.

The city can trace its roots back to 1000 BCE when a Phoenician trading post was established. By the end of the thirteenth century, Plymouth was the main base in England for campaigns against France and in 1295, Edward I gathered England's first national navy there, with a fleet of 325 ships. By the mid-fourteenth century Plymouth had become the fourth largest town in England, exceeded only by London, Bristol and York. The town exported fish, tin, woollen goods, and lead; imports included wine, fruit, sugar, onions and garlic. Sporadic raids by the French in the early fifteenth century led Henry V to order a strengthening of defences and construction of a castle to oversee the entrance to Sutton Harbour. In 1691 the construction of a dockyard began, and as it expanded so did the town surrounding it; initially known as Plymouth Dock and later as Devonport. Within 100 years the dockyard had become one of the world's foremost naval arsenals. The Crimean War in the 1850s and the Boer War at the end of the nineteenth century brought further expansion, and during the First World War the workforce of the dockyard increased to 20,000. There were cutbacks during the depression of the inter-war period but the Second World War increased the workforce again. However the importance of Plymouth as a naval base led to devastation

	Males	Females	Total	Females as % of Total Population	Increase in Population (%)
1801	18016	25178	43194	58.3	-
1811	-	-	56060	-	29.8
1821	26457	34755	61212	56.8	9.2
1831	-	-	75534	-	23.4
1841	35056	45003	80059	56.2	6.0
1851	46806	55574	102380	54.3	27.9
1861	62332	65050	127382	51.1	24.4
1871	63692	69175	132867	52.1	4.3
1881	65757	72086	137843	52.3	3.7
1891	75605	78852	154457	51.1	12.1
1901	95855	97329	193184	50.4	25.1
1911	103176	104280	207456	50.3	7.4
1921	104280	105756	210036	50.4	1.2
1931	102196	105986	208182	50.9	-0.9

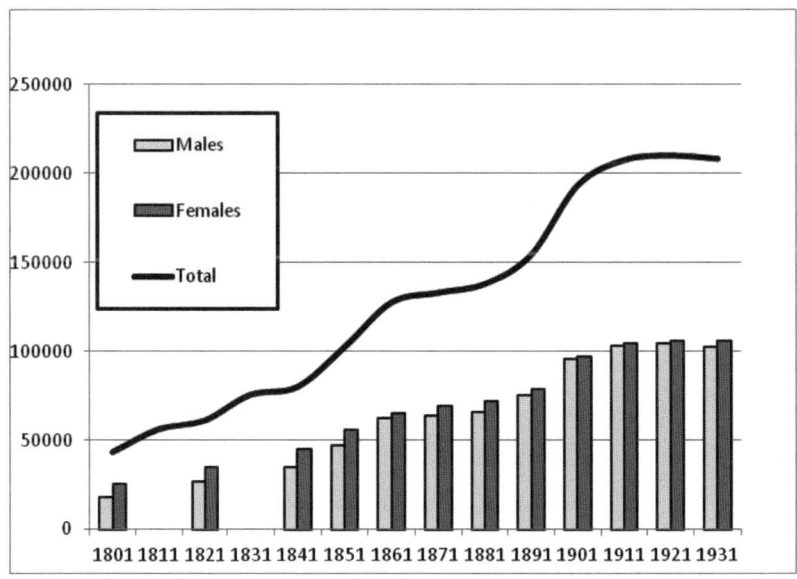

Fig. 1.2: Population Changes in the Three Towns

during the Plymouth Blitz. HMNB Devonport is still the largest naval base in Western Europe and the population of Plymouth today stands at over 260,000.

Plymouth's importance as a dockyard and naval base and its maritime role undeniably affected its population and their livelihoods. The growing dockyard at Devonport meant a rapid increase in population and the Three Towns were beset with problems of poor housing, overcrowding and disease. Figure 1.2 shows the changes in population over the period, taken from census records.

The higher proportion of females in the population is clear and earlier travellers to Plymouth remarked on it being a 'town of women.'[1] The dominance of the dockyard as an employer created particular issues for these women. There were few other large industries in the area and employment opportunities tended to be limited to the domestic service and textiles industries, creating a significant population of poor and unemployed women. This, in conjunction with the large and transient population of military and seafaring men, caused some of the town's more colourful features. The problems of prostitution and disease led to Plymouth being one of the first areas to be targeted by the controversial Contagious Diseases Acts of the 1860s and organised opposition to the Acts played an important part in the fledgling feminist and suffrage movements.

CHAPTER 2

Prostitution and Protest: Plymouth and the Contagious Diseases Acts

'We are not beasts of the field...'

The Three Towns came to the forefront in the battle to repeal the controversial Contagious Diseases (CD) Acts of the 1860s. Introduced in an attempt to control the venereal disease epidemic raging in the army and navy, the CD Acts laid the blame entirely at the feet of prostitutes. With an unenviable reputation as the VD capital of the country,[1] the Three Towns were among the first to be targeted. The Acts authorised police to arrest any woman suspected of being a prostitute, examine her for disease and detain her in a hospital lock ward. From their introduction in 1864 to final repeal in 1886 the CD Acts caused a storm of public debate plus the spectacle of respectable middle-class women openly discussing prostitution and sexuality. The participation of these women in the repeal campaign helped fan the flames of an emerging feminist movement.

Prostitution in the Three Towns

With the expansion of the dockyards, the Three Towns experienced considerable population growth during the nineteenth century. Drawn in from surrounding villages and towns, men found work in the large casual-labour force of the docks, but opportunities for women were more limited. With so many men at sea, in areas of the 'town of women', three out of five adults were female.[2] Women married to seafaring men could find themselves in dire financial straits. Until 1877 there was no legal obligation for a soldier or sailor to provide for his dependants and the men often received no pay in advance of a voyage to reduce the risk of them jumping ship. Instead they would be paid on return to home port, but this left their dependants without an income. Women seeking employment were mainly limited to domestic service or the textile/laundry trades and the work was irregular and poorly paid. Married women could appeal to the Poor Laws for financial assistance but single women had no such recourse. With the workhouse as the only other option, women turned to any means of earning a living. A prostitute might earn more in a day than a laundry woman could in a week and with new ships constantly docking and a large turnover of transient men, there was a steady supply of customers. In the spring of 1871, forty per cent of single women aged 15–29 who resided alone in lodgings in Plymouth were registered prostitutes.[3] The 1871 census shows a number of women living in Fore Street who listed 'prostitute' as their occupation. At number 78 were Mary Beval and Emma Oliver. Also present on census night was a corporal of the 2nd Regiment whose name is registered as 'UK' or unknown. At number 79 were Mary Luscombe, Miss Blight (just 19) and Eliza Davis and her infant son. A gunner and a private of the 75th Regiment were also present, again names registered as 'unknown'.

Long before the CD Acts came into effect the local authorities in the Three Towns had identified prostitution as a threat to public health and decency. Castle Street, or 'Damnation Alley', was notorious for frequent street brawls and lined with inns and brothels. Under new licensing acts in the 1860s the area was cleared, but with the completion of Millbay docks to the west, prostitutes simply relocated, moving to the Octagon area of Plymouth. The district became so disreputable that in Union Street, respectable ladies would only walk along the south side; the north pavement being reserved for their 'fallen' sisters.[4] A popular meeting place was under the railway bridge.

Union Street, Plymouth c.1920 – Notorious haunt of prostitutes in the nineteenth century. (South West Image Bank)

HOUSE OF MERCY FOR THE FALLEN.

ST. STEPHEN'S HOME, DEVONPORT, offers a shelter to some of the very large number of fallen women who abound in this Garrison and Naval Town. So many desire to give up their life of misery and shame, that the applications for admission are incessant, and on two successive days reached 13 in number. It constantly shelters about 17. The number is limited by the accommodation, and varies as the funds. All will be most thankfully received in Money, Clothes for under garments, Bed Linen, Broken Meat, Books for the Library, or in orders for Laundry Work or Plain Sewing, to be executed by the inmates. Officers in the Army and Navy are especially appealed to. It is hoped that no one will hesitate to contribute because the sum must be small.—Address Mrs. Geo. Mason, or Rev. Geo. Mason, 39, George Street, Devonport; or the Rev. G. W. Procter, Incumbent of St. Stephen's, Devonport.

St Stephens House of Mercy Rescue Home, 8 May 1860. (Western Morning News)

Charitable institutions were established to 'reclaim' prostitutes in rescue homes and female penitentiaries, and there were several orphan asylums that took in destitute girls and trained them to become domestic servants. But prostitution was a major problem for the Three Towns.

Introduction of the Contagious Diseases Acts

Following the Crimean War, the physical health of the military became a grave concern. The 1862 Report of the Committee on the Prevalence of Venereal Disease in the Army and Navy showed that one third of all servicemen were diseased. Naval ports and garrison towns such as Portsmouth and Plymouth had the highest number of cases and prostitutes were blamed – 'these women who keep up the disease and recklessly spread it'.[5] The continental system of registering and examining prostitutes was considered and a committee, which included Florence Nightingale, was established to look at the problem. Nightingale was vehemently opposed to the continental system, considering it nothing more than licensed vice. Instead the committee recommended better leisure opportunities for the men, private washing facilities and the establishment of lock hospitals for VD patients on a voluntary basis. But the cost to the military of dealing with diseased servicemen was significant and there was no confidence that the armed forces could work as celibate 'moral institutions'. In 1864 the government passed the Contagious Diseases Act with amendments in 1866 and 1869, each of which gave extended powers. Plymouth, Portsmouth and Chatham were the first towns to be targeted.

The Contagious Diseases Acts in Plymouth

The Royal Albert Hospital in Devonport, completed in 1863, was a direct result of cooperation between the Admiralty, which wanted a lock ward for prostitutes, and Devonport Dispensary, which wanted a hospital. Thomas Woollcombe, an enthusiastic supporter of the proposed CD Acts and chair of the Dispensary

Committee, facilitated the construction of the hospital and the Admiralty provided significant funding. Florence Nightingale was consulted on the ward layout, although letters from her written in 1861 indicate her reservations over the plans. She was blunt in her criticism of everything from the position of the kitchens beneath the sick wards to the unnecessary size of the surgical ward, and was particularly concerned over the proposed combination of a general with a lock hospital, her objections to the proposed CD Acts already made clear. Apparently only minor amendments were made following her criticism and she did not see the revised plans.[6] A voluntary system was trialled in the lock wards prior to the first CD Act but in a paper read before the Medical Society of University College London it was considered to be a failure; it only reached a small amount of disease and twenty-five per cent of women left uncured. When a new ship docked the lock wards would empty.

The passing of the CD Acts was welcomed by the local authorities and many residents of the Three Towns as a means to deal with the problem of prostitution. Inspector Silas Anniss led the small group of dockyard metropolitan police (the 'water police') authorised by the Acts to arrest women whom they suspected of being prostitutes. The women were examined by a doctor (usually a naval or army surgeon) and if found to be diseased, detained in a local hospital lock ward and treated for a period of up to nine months until cured. If a proven prostitute was found to be clear of disease during the initial examination, she would be registered and required to attend examination every two weeks for as long as she continued her trade. If she refused to be examined then she would be brought before a magistrate and could be imprisoned for up to three months.

In January 1869, Barley House Institution for Fallen Women gave its annual report, as reported in the *Western Morning News*. The Institution claimed that the CD Acts not only restored women's health, but gave them time while in the lock ward to reflect on their lives. Between April 1865 and September 1868, 962 women passed through the lock ward and of those, 366 were reclaimed from prostitution. Barley House either returned the women to their families, found them positions in service or moved them away to start a new life.

Other reports in the newspapers focused on the diminishing levels of disease in the Three Towns. Devonport was held up as the great success of the Acts, with disease among both prostitutes and servicemen reduced, brothels all but eradicated and the streets cleaner and safer.

The 1871 census gives a snapshot of the lock ward at the Royal Albert Hospital at the height of the CD Acts. On the day of the census, seventy-seven women were in the ward. Only one of the women, Amelia Gleeson, was married and two were widowed, Elizabeth Harding and Jane Smith, who was also the oldest woman in the ward at 47. The youngest was aged just 16 and forty of the women were aged 20 or younger. Two of the women had their babies with them.

The lock wards were kept separate from the main hospital and in shared areas such as the chapel, a curtain hid them from other patients. Within the lock ward there was an attempt to segregate 'first cases' from the feared corrupting influence of the more hardened prostitutes. The women did the laundry for the hospital, took on sewing work for a shop in Devonport and made their own dresses.

Caroline Nicholson, a retired Plymouth schoolteacher and passionate opponent of the Acts, wrote a number of pamphlets exposing their working. In May 1873 she visited the lock ward, incensed at reports given to Parliament that no effective rescue work had been carried out in the Three Towns prior to the Acts. As a rescue worker herself she had assisted the former Matron, Miss Bull, when the lock ward was run on a voluntary basis. Her indignity over the Acts and sympathy for the girls detained is clear. She talks of the hypocrisy of listening to the chaplain denouncing the sin of fornication while being in the pay of an Admiralty who claimed it was impossible to maintain a celibate army without fornication. She refuted the claim that a high proportion of the women were 'reclaimed', supported by Miss Bull who believed that less than five per cent of those 'rescued' by the Acts were permanently reclaimed.

Opposition to the Acts

On 13 July 1870, Devonport Petty Sessions considered the case of Harriet Hicks, who had petitioned to be released from the Royal Albert Hospital lock ward. The defence claimed that Hicks was not a prostitute, was not diseased and had never knowingly signed a voluntary submission form giving the authorities permission to examine and detain her. Although previously a prostitute, she had been living with one man, Ebenezer Simmons, for several years, but seven weeks prior to the court case, Inspector Anniss had entered their room and demanded Hicks on information she was diseased. After hearing evidence, including the inability of the medical officer to prove that Hicks was suffering from disease, the court ordered Hicks's immediate discharge.

The petition of Harriet Hicks was a test case for those calling for repeal of the CD Acts and its success led to further resistance – over the summer months of 1870, twenty-nine women came before magistrates in the Three Towns claiming violations under the Acts.[7] The case also served to highlight the many abuses that the repeal campaign claimed – police barging into rooms to arrest women with little or no evidence, medical officers detaining women on unclear diagnoses of disease and the misuse of the voluntary submission form.

When the Acts were first passed, despite the concern of many, there was no organised opposition. However, in 1867 reports of reduction in disease and improved moral standing in subjected areas led to a proposal to extend the Acts to the civilian population in northern towns and unease began to grow over their increased powers. Opposition gathered pace at a meeting of the Social Sciences Congress in Bristol in 1869. Paul Swain of the Royal Albert Hospital presented a paper which supported the Acts and detailed the benefits to the Three Towns. The audience contained numerous opponents (although women were excluded) and newspapers reported that the meeting became a 'bear garden', finally resolving by a large majority to oppose the Acts. Shortly afterwards the National

Association for the Repeal of the Contagious Diseases Act (NA) formed. Initially excluded, women formed the Ladies National Association (LNA) and member Elizabeth Wolstenhulme contacted Josephine Butler, who was already active in calls for the higher education of women and in rescue work. She emerged as a charismatic and persuasive leader of the repeal campaign.

In 1870 the LNA published the 'Ladies Protest' in the *Daily News*, signed by 124 women, including Florence Nightingale. The protest stated that the Acts:

> Violate the legal safeguards enjoyed by women in common with men, they allow police absolute power over women, they punish the sex who are victims of vice and leave unpunished the sex who are the main cause of vice and its dreaded consequence.

The repeal campaign began to arouse strong popular feeling, even in the subjected districts despite the support of the local authorities for the Acts. On 13 June 1870, a Conference of Gentlemen met at the Mechanic's Institute in Plymouth and signed a petition to present to both Houses of Parliament asking for the total repeal of the Acts. In the same month, Josephine Butler spoke at both Devonport and Plymouth at meetings attended by many working class women. She talked of how figures showing the success of the Acts had been distorted and that claims of a reduced number of prostitutes did not stand close scrutiny and made no account of the number of women now operating clandestinely. With the suffrage campaign still in its infancy, the spectacle of women speaking at large public meetings was unusual. Supporters of the Acts were particularly hostile to these 'ladies' who openly discussed such intimate subjects. Some newspapers were supportive; *The Spectator* wrote, 'it gives us a new ideal of women's intellectual courage and capacity for political life'. Others were less generous – the *Saturday Review* referred to the LNA as the 'Shrieking Sisterhood'.

Branches of the both the NA and LNA formed in the Three Towns with members coming from the non-conformist and

Quaker sections of the community, including Alfred Balkwill, a Plymouth Quaker and his cousins the Bragg sisters who would later be involved in the suffrage campaign. Middle-class women worked with paid working-class agents to organise public meetings and explain the opposition to the Acts. One of the biggest issues was the 'double standard' in that blame for the spread of disease was aimed purely at women and ignored the contribution of men. The repeal campaign claimed that the Acts were intended to create a workforce of disease-free women and tacitly accepted that men would continue to use prostitutes. A report into the working of the Acts, commissioned in 1871, took just this view that prostitution was a necessary evil, stating that:

> There is no comparison to be made between prostitutes and the men who consort with them. With the one sex the offence committed is a matter of gain; with the other it is an irregular indulgence of a natural inclination.

There was particular concern over the definition of a 'common prostitute', and fear that the police could accuse any woman who was in the wrong place at the wrong time. Stories began to circulate of respectable women being harassed by the police when they were simply making their way home from work along darkened streets. To arrest a woman the police were supposed to have several concurrent proofs that she was a prostitute, but these 'proofs' were vague and included being informed on by servicemen or other prostitutes, with no acknowledgement that these accusations could be malicious or mistaken. Supporters of the Acts maintained that virtuous women were not at risk and neither were immoral women as long as their immorality was not publicly practised. However, evidence suggested otherwise. Douglas Kingsford produced a critical summary of the Acts for the repeal campaign, which suggested that the rules of proof were interpreted very differently by individuals. In Devonport, Mr Sloggett, the examining surgeon would not consider a woman a common prostitute if 'she went with a man on only one or two occasions', whereas Inspector Anniss would immediately bring in a woman who 'received men in a private way in her own house'.

The 1866 CD Act included a new clause requiring the periodic examination of all registered prostitutes, whether they were diseased or not, extending the power the police had over a much larger group of women. Inspector Anniss was championed by supporters of the Acts in the Three Towns but opponents saw him as cold, authoritarian and arrogant, not above bending the laws and with no sympathy for working-class women.[8] Kingsford's critical summary gave evidence of the water police acting as little more than spies and stretching their brief to the limit. In Devonport, they were reported to have called at the house of a girl of 16 several times in one day to bring her in for examination. The girl's mother provided proof from a private doctor that she was innocent but the publicity caused by the police meant she was subjected to taunts and suspicion. In another case, four sisters were ordered to attend examination, but all refused. After one of the girls had an evening out, the police again called at the house and detailed every place she had visited, showing that she had been under surveillance. The girls again refused to attend examination and no further action was taken, suggesting that the police had no evidence against them, but the girls were subsequently called after in the street, so much so that their mother appealed to the police for protection. There are other tales of the water police bursting into women's rooms, checking under the bedcovers for men and ordering women to get dressed in front of them to attend examination. The repeal campaign maintained that innocent women and girls caught up in the Acts had their reputations ruined and found it impossible to gain honest employment. Others who attended examination or were detained in the lock wards lost their accommodation, with landlords throwing them out once word of their situation had spread.

There were two examination rooms in the Three Towns, one at the Royal Albert Hospital and the other in Flora Lane, Plymouth, above which Inspector Anniss lived. Women attending for examination ran a gauntlet of taunts and insults from those living nearby and the surrounding inns were generally full of servicemen on examination day. Graphic literature was produced to show the pain and degradation of the examination. Women were known to get drunk beforehand in order to cope with it, some left the district and others preferred the choice of prison rather than submit to it. Supporters of the Acts scorned the view that the examination was degrading, asking whether 'a woman who might be visited by several men each day could actually be capable of further degradation'. Again the double standard was raised – examinations for servicemen had been dropped in 1857 because the men found it demoralising, yet women were supposed to have no such feelings. The repeal campaign also pointed out that the examining surgeons who claimed that women were neither humiliated nor discomfited by the procedure were appointed and paid by the Admiralty and War Office – the very body which wanted to uphold the Acts. The competence of these examining surgeons, often naval surgeons with no experience of disease in women, was questioned. In 1868 and 1869, surgeons at the Royal Albert Hospital received several cases where no evidence of disease could be found.

A tactic of the LNA was to agitate among prostitutes. In 1870, Eliza Binney from Plymouth had been certified as suffering from disease and ordered to go immediately to the lock ward. She was stopped by two repeal agents, Elizabeth King and Daniel Cooper, who informed Binney that she should not go unless she had signed a voluntary submission form. A scuffle broke out involving Inspector Anniss and both King and Cooper were arrested. Binney was taken to the hospital, found not to be suffering from disease and released, but was still subject to the fortnightly examinations. At trial both King and Cooper were found guilty and fined £5. Eliza Binney had been a known prostitute after an inquest into the death of a visitor to her brothel in 1869 – ironically, the visitor had been a naval surgeon. In another case the *WMN* of 15 October 1870 described the arrest of repeal agent John Marshall for unlawfully obstructing the metropolitan police in the execution of their duties. He incited a prostitute, Sarah Mach, to resist arrest and was sentenced to two month's hard labour. At the trial Sarah Mach was asked if she had been bribed to speak in Marshall's defence. She defended her integrity and said, 'I think we are allowed to know our own feelings. We are not beasts of the field.'[9]

The LNA were particularly concerned with the system of voluntary submission forms. If signed by a woman, these forms gave their permission for examination without the police having to provide evidence of prostitution. A woman was within her rights to refuse to sign but there was evidence of women being coerced by erroneous threats of prison if they did not. There was no procedure to ensure the women fully understood what they were signing and there were cases of illiterate women being made to sign forms they could not read with an 'X'. Once women were discharged from hospital they were presumed to have given up prostitution and if police wanted to arrest them again then new forms would need to be signed or new evidence found. In practice the police often held the old forms and reused them, or forced women to sign new forms before they were released from hospital. The LNA gave women advice, legal defence and moral support and produced pamphlets which explained the working of the Acts and women's rights. LNA member Mary Hume-Rothery recalled distributing pamphlets to a group of women leaving the examination room at Devonport. She reported in the LNA publication *The Shield*, that she was touched to see the women consulting the pamphlets together:

> One girl sprang up and threw a copy into the hospital yard, perhaps hoping that it might reach one of the women detained inside.

On the Brink of Failure

Despite popular campaigning, repeal Bills presented to Parliament throughout the 1870s had no success but the government did set up a Royal Commission to look into the working of the Acts in 1871. Only one member, Robert Applegarth, suggested that the committee actually speak to prostitutes. He visited Devonport where he became convinced that women were being abused. However, of twenty-three committee members, Applegarth was one of only four opposed to the Acts and the result was their endorsement by the Commission. Eleven members did recommend that the periodic examination of disease-free women be abolished but the government failed to act on this point. By 1874, and with a Conservative government in power, repeal campaigning in the subjected districts, including the Three Towns, had stalled.

In 1876 there was an attempt to re-ignite the campaign. A Plymouth and Devonport League for the Repeal of the CD Acts was formed and in February 1877 two public meetings were held. But support for the Acts still ran high and both meetings were hijacked, with resolutions passed in favour of the Acts. The LNA of the Three Towns continued efforts with a series of public and drawing-room meetings, but these were described by the *WMN* in April 1877 in less than flattering terms:

> A series of meetings 'for women only' are about to be held at which there will be no check of misstatements, no fear of opposing arguments and from whose wholly one-sided gatherings petitions may be sent to Parliament as the voice of 'the women of Plymouth'.

Increasingly, repeal efforts in the Three Towns moved away from political activity and towards rescue work. John Marshall and his wife ran a rescue home and were involved in an underground railway which spirited women away from Plymouth. But a new wave of rescue work arrived with the social-purity movement and Ellice Hopkins who came to Plymouth to establish an industrial school for girls. Although she resented the double-standard of the Acts, she did not connect prostitution with the economic difficulties of women, instead she espoused morality and chastity. She roused a great sense of duty in Plymouth to the work of rescuing fallen women and preventing young girls from 'falling' in the first place and this played into the hands of supporters of the Acts who formed their own Plymouth Friendless Girls' Association. The association received the assistance of the water police who helped them track down girls on the brink of prostitution. John Marshall lost much of the support for his own rescue work and left Plymouth in 1880.

In 1879 another government inquiry was commissioned. This committee gave its report in 1882 which, to the dismay of the repeal campaign, again supported the Acts, dismissing evidence of police abuse as malicious propaganda. James Stansfield, a major supporter of the repeal campaign, was one of a minority of six who rejected official statistics on the success of the Acts. But, despite the conclusion of the committee, all was not lost. In 1882, Stansfield was returned to the Cabinet and some saw this as Prime Minister Gladstone's tacit support for repeal. Finally, in April 1883, Stansfield moved that:

> The House disapproves of the compulsory examination
> of women under the Contagious Diseases Acts.

The motion was carried by 182 votes to 111, despite vehement objections from the local authorities in subjected districts, and meant that the periodic examination of women was stopped. Without this the Acts were effectively crippled and were suspended. They were finally repealed in 1886.

The Legacy of the Acts

The political make-up of both opponent and support groups of the Acts was complex but both sides were in some ways guilty of failing to understand the economic and social conditions which led women into prostitution. Many opposed the Acts, not because they sympathised with the prostitutes, but because they saw them as condoning a vice which should be eradicated. It was a fine line between solidarity with prostitutes and condemnation of them for their actions. One of Butler's strengths was her genuine respect and sympathy for the working classes and she maintained that poverty, not sin, forced women onto the streets. This contrasts to a pamphlet published in 1882 by an ex-constable of Devonport which maintained that:

> Women enter prostitution for pleasure and vanity, not out of economic necessity, and attractive women of the lower classes are almost exclusively of low character and likely to engage in clandestine prostitution.

Suspicions were that this was written by Inspector Anniss.[10]

The importance of the LNA was not only the part it played in the eventual repeal of the CD Acts, but in the opportunity it offered for women to work together. The Acts came at a time when the feminist movement was in its early stages and women were beginning to question their oppression at the hands of men and government. The members of the LNA leadership were involved in an array of causes. Seventeen prominent suffragists served on the LNA executive and others were involved in reform groups looking at higher education, married women's rights and employment. Through the LNA, women were exposed to political campaigning and addressing large public meetings. They protested over the Acts both in the courts and on the streets and there was some surprise over the vehemence and success of their actions. At the time of the campaign, women were still greatly constrained by views over the limitations of their sex and the courage of both the women of the LNA and the women they were fighting for should not be underestimated.

CHAPTER 3

Educating Girls

*'Educated girls are better mothers and have more chance
at marriage...'*

The Push for Women's Education

Education in the early nineteenth century was heavily influenced
by class and gender. Few working-class children regularly
attended school. Education was neither compulsory nor free and
many families relied on the income from their children's labour.
The 1802 Health and Morals of Apprentices Act required mills
and factories to provide a basic education for apprentices, many
of whom were young pauper children, but there was no means
of enforcement.

Education for middle- and upper-class boys prepared
them for university, the professions or the army, but for girls
the situation was very different. Women were not expected to
work; instead their education concentrated on social etiquette
and preparation for domesticity. Girls tended to be taught
at home by governesses who were often not well educated
themselves. There were fears that education might cause a girl
to develop academic aspirations which would undermine her
domestic role, or that it could strain her delicate constitution.
A condition called 'anorexia scholastica' was coined by the
medical profession who believed debilitating weakness and
thinness could be caused by too much mental stimulus. Victorian
philosopher and sociologist Herbert Spencer theorised that
female intellectual evolution stopped earlier than in males,
to prepare women for childbirth. Excessive study could cause
infertility.

1802	Health and Morals of Apprentices Act: mills and factories to provide a basic education for young apprentices
1861	Newcastle Report: examines provision of education for the working classes
1868	Taunton Report: examines secondary education provision
1869	Endowed Schools Act: extends provision of endowments to girls
1870	Elementary Education Act: creation of school boards
1874	Plymouth High School for Girls established
1882	London University opens degrees to men and women
1891	Elementary Education Act: elementary schooling is made free of charge
1892	First woman elected on to Plymouth school board
1899	Elementary Education Act: compulsory school age raised to 12
1902	Education Act: abolishes school boards and creates Local Education Authorities
1908	Devonport Secondary School for Girls established
1919	Sex Disqualification (Removal) Act: universities are permitted to award degrees to women
1920	Oxford University awards degrees to women
1944	Education Act (the Butler Act): overhauls all previous legislation. All children aged 5–15 have the right to a free education
1948	Cambridge University awards degrees to women
1996	Education Act: repeals previous legislation

Fig. 3.1: Education Timeline

Towards the middle of the nineteenth century however women began to set their sights on educational reform as a means to change women's lives and give them equal opportunities with men.

Education in the Three Towns

The Three Towns, as elsewhere, had a variety of schools:

Dame Schools were run by working-class women in their own homes, taught a basic curriculum of reading, writing and arithmetic and emphasised domestic skills for girls. In 1871 it was estimated that 1,000 children attended Dame schools in Plymouth.

Ragged Schools were charity run and provided free education and often food and clothing for the children of those too poor to pay. In 1861, Plymouth's ragged schools were included in an inquiry which concluded that they were ineffective, fostered criminality and provided a poor education. Half of the pupils attending were found to have dissolute parents who would rather spend their money on drink than education and it was suggested that these children should not be accommodated. Supporters of ragged schools argued that such parents would simply leave their children to roam the streets – at least ragged schools gave them a chance at education. Parents' views on girls' education were also sought during the inquiry and the overall conclusion was that, while some parents were keen for their daughters to be educated, this was so:

> They would make better mothers, have more chance at marriage and be more interesting companions to their husbands.

Elementary schools catered for children from 6 to 12 and were privately or church run, charging fees of around one penny per week. Churches also ran Sunday schools for children and adults. Notre Dame School was opened in 1865 by the Sisters of Notre Dame, a religious congregation founded in 1804 by two French women. Dedicated to the education of girls, they believed that education should be for all no matter the ability of the child.

Reformatory and Industrial schools and Orphan Asylums provided accommodation and education for young offenders, orphans and neglected children, with a particular emphasis on keeping girls from prostitution. Plymouth Girls Industrial

St Budeaux Sunday School c.1920. (South West Image Bank)

Home was certified in 1883 and run by Matron, Mrs Bacon. The school could take forty girls aged 8–14, and some were placed there by magistrates. The girls were prepared for life in domestic service. The Royal British Female Orphan Asylum, Devonport, was specifically for orphans of servicemen and took girls aged 7–13 to train them for domestic service. One pupil of the asylum left a detailed account of her time at the school. The anonymous author entered the orphanage in 1907 at the age of 7. Her father, a bandsman in the 2nd Dorsets, had died, leaving her mother with eight children. On arrival her hair was cropped and she was bathed and dressed in the orphanage uniform. A typical day involved rising at 6 a.m. to wash in cold water, then housework before breakfast (porridge or bread and dripping) at 8 a.m. After prayers, the morning was taken up with reading, writing and arithmetic. A cooked meal was served at noon followed by some time for play, then sewing and knitting. School finished at 4 p.m. when, if it was fine, the girls took a walk before tea. Older girls began their domestic service training until ready for service at 16. Although the work was hard, the writer remembers that they had fun. Every Christmas there was a gift for each girl and staff prepared and served the Christmas meal. They always attended the launching of a ship from Devonport and there were trips out to Mount Edgcumbe House where they had donkey rides. Relatives could visit once a month and the girls were allowed one day out each year with surviving parents and relatives. They looked forward to these, even though they were dunked in a bath as soon as they returned to the orphanage! The home had a resident nurse, a doctor visited every day and a physical fitness instructor came in once a week. They 'were well looked after and never ill-treated'.[1]

The emphasis on training girls for domestic service was to provide them with a respectable occupation and to keep them from the streets, but a survey taken in 1911 showed that forty-six per cent of illegitimate children in Britain were born to domestic servants. The Orphan Asylum did consider training the more intelligent girls as teachers, but in the end rejected the proposal.

Towards Change

During the 1860s, the provision of education throughout the country began to be investigated more thoroughly and there was a campaign by the National Education League (NEL) for compulsory, non-sectarian education. The 1868 Taunton Report examined secondary school provision aimed mostly at the middle classes and included an investigation into the state of girls' education, which found serious weaknesses. Parents were generally indifferent, believing that a girl would be provided for in marriage, girls' secondary schools were few and tended to be small (at the time of the report there were only thirteen in England), teaching was of poor quality and there were significantly fewer endowments for girls than boys.[2]

The 1861 Newcastle Report revealed that older children of the working classes rarely attended school regularly and that much of the education they did receive was poor.

Both of these reports prompted changes. The 1869 Endowed Schools Act attempted to extend the benefits of endowments to girls 'as far as conveniently may be'. More sweeping changes came with the 1870 Education Act, which created School Boards to coordinate the provision of elementary education. Although the intention of the 1870 Act was to increase school attendance, this was not yet made compulsory and the *WMN* of 3 March 1870 reported the views of the Plymouth and Devonport branches of the NEL that the Act failed on three points – not making schools non-sectarian, not making attendance compulsory and not making education free.

Plymouth's first School Board formed in 1871 and determined that Plymouth needed to provide eight new schools. Over the next few years several schools were transferred to the Board, including the King Street and Catte Street Ragged Schools. By the end of 1887, Plymouth had thirteen voluntary schools and ten board schools but they had slightly less accommodation than necessary for girls and infants. Attendance at both voluntary schools and board schools was higher than the nationwide average of sixty per cent.

Further reform followed with a series of Elementary Education Acts. The 1891 Elementary Education Act made all elementary schooling free and by 1899 the compulsory school age was raised to 12. Annual School Board returns gave details such as the numbers on roll, attendance and subjects taught. The return for Castle Street School for the year ended 1894 shows the school had a total of 178 students aged 3–9, and there were slightly more girls attending than boys. The girls were instructed in needlework and cutting-out for two lessons per week. Other school returns show that girls were regularly instructed in household management, cookery, laundry work and dairy work.[3]

There was opposition to the Education Acts. Some feared that encouraging the education of the working classes could lead to their dissatisfaction and the risk of mass revolt. Even those who advocated education for all still felt that the education of girls should be solely to prepare them for their domestic role. On 10 October 1874 a discussion on the Education of Women took place at the Corn Exchange, Plymouth. The *WDM* reported that, although it was agreed that the education of women required development, there were still constraints. Women were the custodians of charity and courtesy and their education should not make them hard and uncaring. Women's education should always be in regard to their social position and duties and its ultimate aim was a woman as prized wife, affectionate mother and accomplished trainer of her children. One speaker admitted that he 'shuddered' at the thought of educated women becoming barristers or doctors.

Higher Education for Girls

Despite such views, as the nineteenth century went on girls were given more opportunity to continue their education into secondary level. Plymouth High School for Girls was established in 1874 and a report in the *WMN* of the school's Speech Day on 7 December 1918 shows how far matters had progressed. The Headmistress paid tribute to the school's success in producing the right kind of girl and that this was apparent in the response they had made to war work. Several former girls were in France and Salonika with the WAAC and WRNS, or were in banks or hospitals or driving cars and ambulances. Four former girls were now training as doctors. The Archdeacon replied that:

> There was room for much more thoroughness in the education of girls. It was quite probable that in the next twenty-five years there would be women preachers and ministers, barristers and social workers of all kinds. He might even be addressing a future Prime Minister.

The following year the Headmistress was again pleased to speak of the success of the school and that it had now formally taken its place as the top rung in the local public educational ladder. She said that:

> The demand for better education was a good sign and as working women now had the vote it was essential that

the best brains amongst the working class girls should have the same opportunity as boys for climbing the educational ladder.

The 1902 Education Act abolished School Boards and created Local Education Authorities. It standardised the education system and led to a rapid growth of secondary schools, including nearly 350 girls' schools.

Devonport Secondary School for Girls was established in 1908, initially sited at Devonport Technical College. In October 1918, the Education Committee reported on the school's results in the Cambridge Local Examinations:

> Juniors: 37 presented, 33 successful:– 1 first class honours, 6 third class honours, 26 passes. There were nine distinctions in religious knowledge, history and botany and 15 passed in oral French.

> Seniors: 25 presented, 20 successful:– 1 first class honours, 1 second class honours, 9 third class, 9 passes. There were 11 distinctions in religious knowledge, history, botany, and geography, 5 passed in oral French.

In 1937 a new building was constructed and the school renamed Devonport High School for Girls. The new school was modern for its time and, although there were still large classrooms allocated for needlework and domestic science, the school also had laboratories for chemistry, physics and botany.

The 1944 Education Act replaced almost all previous legislation and set the framework for post-war education. Under the Act, which gave all children aged 5–15 the right to free education, LEAs had to provide separate primary and secondary schools, nursery provision for under fives and to make provision for 'pupils who suffer from any disability of body or mind'; in main schools where possible. The first post-war Minister of Education was Ellen Wilkinson who fought her way to university from working-class roots but sadly committed suicide in 1947 after she felt she had failed to achieve all the

Devonport Technical School, Original Site of Devonport High School for Girls. (South West Image Bank)

reforms necessary. The 1944 Act continued the tripartite system of grammar, technical and secondary modern schools. Access to grammar and selective schools was restricted to those who passed the 11+ exam which tended to favour children of the middle classes. The Act was repealed by the 1996 Education Act.

The push for women to be allowed to graduate from university began during the mid-nineteenth century. Two colleges for the education of girls were founded in Cambridge: Girton College in 1869 and Newnham Hall in 1875. Both had to contend with the view that further education would tempt women away from their natural sphere and pose a threat to family life. In 1874 Henry Maudsley published *Sex and Mind in Education* which argued that women would suffer immense harm to their health if they studied as men did, and in 1886 the British medical profession called for protective legislation of educated women analogous to that of the Factory Acts. In response the colleges carried out research on health, marriage and childbirth patterns of former students. Their findings contradicted medical opinion and concluded that college-educated women were healthier and less likely to have childless marriages.

However, studying at colleges like Girton and Newnham did not mean women received degrees and the women were reliant on supportive academics to give lectures and pass on examinations. In 1882 the University of London was the first to open its degrees to both men and women, and at the turn of the century when many provincial universities were receiving their charters they also opened their doors on equal terms. Oxford and Cambridge were late to the party. The 1919 Sex Disqualification (Removal) Act permitted universities to award degrees to women and although Oxford did so the following year, Cambridge resisted until 1948.

The Education Committee of Plymouth Council discussed university education on 4 March 1918. The view was that throughout the southwest they were lacking the facilities of a university education for young men and women. A university open to all classes and ranks would be an effective contribution to national education and the suggestion was that the college at Exeter be developed further. A notice in the *WMN* of 28 May 1948 announced that a Devonport High School girl had won a scholarship to University College of the South West, now Exeter University. Across the country today, slightly more than fifty per cent of university students are female.

CHAPTER 4

Doctors and Nurses

'Women should nurse, not doctor...'

Women have always been involved in medicine, whether as apothecaries or herbalists, nurses or midwives, doctors or surgeons. Census details for the Three Towns (figure 4.2) show women were employed as nurses and midwives from 1841, but it is not until 1901 that the first female physician is listed.

Nursing and Midwifery

Nursing was an acceptable occupation for women at a time when employment opportunities were limited. The caring aspect certainly fits with the concept of women's sphere, but until the mid-nineteenth century nursing was also believed to require neither skill nor training, and the work was casual and poorly paid. In Florence Nightingale's words, nursing was left to 'those who were too old, too weak, too drunken, too dirty, too stupid or too bad to do anything else'.[1] But the actions of Nightingale and Mary Seacole during the Crimean War, together with medical advances began to raise the profile of the profession. Nightingale's insistence on sanitary conditions and Seacole's care of wounded officers at her 'British Hotel' significantly reduced the number of deaths, while the increased treatment of patients in hospitals required higher levels of nursing skill. From the 1860s, training schools for nurses were established and the British Nurses Association was created in 1887. At the start of the twentieth century, the health of the nation became of greater concern – even more so during and after the First World War. Breakthroughs in treatment and

1854	Florence Nightingale travels to Turkey to lead a team of nurses during the Crimean War
1855	Mary Seacole opens her British Hotel for convalescent soldiers in the Crimean War
1865	Elizabeth Garrett Anderson becomes the first practising English female doctor
1867	Joseph Lister publishes Antiseptic Principles of the Practice of Surgery
1876	British Medical Act authorises British Medical Association to licence all qualified applicants no matter their gender
1887	British Nurses Association Established
1892	British Medical Association accepts female doctors
1899	Felix Hoffman Develops Aspirin
1902	Queen Alexandra's Imperial Military Nursing Service established Midwives Act: This and subsequent acts ensured stricter guidelines in assuring only qualified midwives could attend births
1916	Royal College of Nursing founded
1918	Midwives Act
1919	Nurses Registration Act
1926	Midwives Act
1928	Sir Alexander Fleming discovers penicillin
1936	Midwives Act
1946	National Health Service Act
1951	Male nurses allowed to join professional register
1953	Watson & Crick discover structure of DNA molecule

Fig. 4.1: Healthcare Timeline

surgery meant that more could now be done for more illnesses and injuries and with improvements in medicine came further improvements in standards of care. In 1916 the College of Nursing was established and in 1919 the Nurses Registration

	1841		1851		1861		1871		1881ᵃ		1891		1901		1911		1921	
	M	F	M	F	M	F	M	F	M	F	M	F	M	F	M	F	M	F
Physician/Surgeon/GP	139	-	112	-	82	-	86	-	13	-	93	-	120	1	98	2	148	6
Nurse	-	155	-	271	-	211	-	195	-	181	3	329	35	280	6	487	9	527
Midwifeᵇ	-	3	-	6	-	2	-	8	-	5	-	-	-	19	-	-	-	29
Domestic Service Nurseᶜ	-	-	-	131	-	311	-	319	-	-	-	-	-	-	-	-	-	-
Dentistᵈ	-	-	-	-	16	-	20	-	26	-	36	-	-	-	-	-	62	4
Vetᵈ	-	-	-	-	-	-	-	-	-	-	10	-	-	-	-	-	5	-

ᵃ1881 figures are for Plymouth only
ᵇ1891 and 1911 figures for midwives are included in the total for nurses
ᶜDomestic service nurses are not listed separately from 1881
ᵈNo separate figures for dentist or vet were listed in 1901 or 1911

Fig. 4.2: No. of Male and Female Medical Professionals in the Three Towns

Act established the General Nursing Council and required the registration of nurses. The 1902 Midwives Act, plus successive Acts in 1918, 1926 and 1936, improved midwifery standards and ensured that midwives were also trained and registered.

Formal nurse training began at the South Devon and East Cornwall Hospital at the start of the twentieth century. Training lasted for four years and nurses had to pass three exams. At the start of the First World War the hospital employed fifty nurses under the control of Matron Harriet Hopkins, a member of the General Nursing Council. Much of the selection of new nurses was based on whether matron considered them to be from a respectable background, with the moral values that she demanded. In 1913 the *WMN* published a letter from a publican who objected to the rejection of his daughter's nursing application on the grounds that she would have to wear her uniform to the inn on her return home. Matron had thought it would detract from the dignity of the profession. Successful applicants included the daughters of a vicar and a senior surgeon. The trainee nurses were encouraged to aspire to a middle-class lifestyle and were provided with a croquet set, lawn tennis court and a library. They worked an average of sixty hours a week with one full day and two half days off. Their routine involved lots of cleaning and washing of both wards and patients and the relatively new system of regular patient monitoring.

The 1924-25 Annual Report of the Devon and Cornwall Training School and Home for Nurses and Three Towns

Nursing Association and Maternity Home in Stonehouse gives some details of nurses' lives. The training school was to:

> Provide training for nurses and skilled nursing for the sick poor and working classes in their own homes without distinction of creed.

The nurses received strict instructions on dos and don'ts:

- *Nurses are strictly forbidden to interfere in any way with the religious opinions of their patients or members of their families.*
- *Nurses shall not accept presents from patients or their families.*
- *Nurses shall be responsible for any appliances or clothing lent to their patients and see as far as possible that they are returned in good condition.*
- *Nurses are responsible for the personal cleanliness of their patients. They shall endeavour to improve their personal surroundings and when the relative can be taught how to keep the room in nursing order they should be encouraged to do so.*

Of thirty-nine pupils entered for the exam of the Central Midwives Board all but three had passed at first sitting and the remaining three were expected to pass at the second. A recent inspection by the Queen Victoria's Jubilee Institute for Nurses had recorded that:

> The work seen with district nurses and in the maternity home was very satisfactory, the methods good and home visits greatly appreciated. The training sisters were painstaking in teaching and supervision. The infant welfare and ante-natal clinics were well used. Patients past and present of the maternity home spoke of its value and the kindness and comfort they received there and the home received many letters of thanks. The service was increasingly used by mothers who would otherwise be attended by midwives in their own homes.[2]

By the end of the Second World War there was a shortage of nurses and there were attempts to attract more women to the service by improved working conditions. The *WMN* of 16 November 1945 reported that nurses were being offered higher wages, four weeks holiday and the promise of no more scrubbing due to the plan to employ domestic staff to clean wards. Over 2,000 girls in the forces were being offered immediate release if they agreed to train as nurses. Other incentives included the removal of the marriage bar and allowing nurses to live at home, as long as they could still provide the required level of service.

Female Doctors in Plymouth

By the beginning of the nineteenth century women had effectively been excluded from becoming doctors by the requirement for university training. This was not a deterrent for all; Margaret Bulkley disguised herself as a man, obtained a medical degree from Edinburgh University in 1812, and practised as army surgeon 'James Barry' for over forty years without detection.

The rising feminist movement of the mid-nineteenth century included the call for women to be able to enter the professions, including medicine. Elizabeth Garrett Anderson became the first practising English female doctor in 1865 by sitting exams with the Society of Apothecaries, which did not explicitly exclude women. The following year the Society closed the loophole and refused to examine any candidate who had not studied at a recognised medical school. Undaunted, women continued to campaign, declaring that not only were they capable of becoming doctors, but that many women would prefer a female doctor, especially in maternity matters. The 1876 Medical Act authorised the British Medical Association to license all qualified applicants no matter their gender, but this did not stop the negative attitudes towards women doctors. It was claimed that women should not be exposed to such intimate subjects given their delicate nature, that they were not up to the mental and physical strain and it would detract from their proper role of wife and mother. In August 1878 the *WMN* recorded medical journal *The Lancet's* objections to women practicing medicine:

> Women were helpmeets for men and should nurse, not doctor. As nurses were distrustful of female doctors, the supply of nurses would cease and men could not nurse as they would not consent to become passive instruments as women would. A woman would not be man's helpmeet if she doctored him and she was never intended to doctor her own sex, for the original intention of her existence was to devote herself to man.

In 1884 the *WMN* reported that *The Lancet* had grudgingly given up its feud with the movement for giving women doctors of their own gender, but it still maintained that male doctors would bar the door to women's education and they would be asked to form their own hospitals and not to interfere with men. However, over the next few years more medical schools began to open their doors to women and in 1892 the British Medical Association finally accepted female doctors. The first female doctor in Plymouth was recorded in the 1901 census, but the appointment of female doctors onto the staff of Plymouth hospitals was a particular issue. On 27 June 1925 the *WMN* reported on a meeting hosted by Dr Ramsay, one of Plymouth's earliest female doctors. Speaker Lady Barrett said that in Plymouth there were a great number of women who would prefer to be treated in hospitals by doctors of their own sex, and the number of women on lady doctors' waiting lists was proof of women's faith in each other. A Women's Hospital Fund (WHF) was to be established to supply hospital beds for such women and would work alongside a campaign to have women doctors appointed at the city's hospitals.

On 21 November 1925 the *WMN* reported that attempts to induce the South Devon and East Cornwall Hospital committee to appoint at least one women doctor on the honorary staff continued. Mrs Ruth Watmough informed the paper that a petition of some 3,500 signatures had been drawn up, including councillors, clergy and business leaders. They requested the appointment of women doctors in charge of beds in the same manner as men, particularly as Plymouth was lagging behind other large towns in this respect.

Four years later at an annual meeting of the WHF the situation had not changed. Speaking, Dr Ramsay said that:

> A Labour government can appoint a woman cabinet minister but so far the conservative medical profession will not appoint a woman doctor on the staff of Plymouth hospitals.

There had been repeated applications for positions but to no avail. Through the WHF, patients were being seen by women doctors at Greenbank Nursing Home with twenty-eight women treated over the past year. Patients had contributed according to their means and fund raising for the WHF continued.

By 1931, frustration was growing and at the annual meeting, Dr Ramsay deplored the fact that the WHF was still a necessity. Thirty-five cases had been seen the previous year at North Friary Nursing Home following the closure of Greenbank and in every case the women were grateful to have received attention from female doctors. In June 1932 the annual meeting agreed that the state of affairs of the voluntary hospitals regarding women doctors was archaic.

Campaigning continued and on 29 May 1933 the Hon. Secretary of the SD&EC Hospital, Mr Hollely, wrote to the *WMN* to say that the push to get a woman doctor on the staff was misleading as the house physician, the officer in charge of the radium department, the assistant pathologist, and at least one anaesthetist were all women. In response, Lilian Charlton, Hon. Secretary of the WHF, clarified that, while the appointment of women into such positions was to be applauded, none of the voluntary hospitals in Plymouth had a woman doctor on the visiting staff and it was only a visiting doctor who had charge of beds. If a patient of a woman doctor had to go to hospital she was immediately turned over to the care of a man, no matter her own desires. She hoped that people would be awakened to the inequality in the treatment of men and women doctors. The WHF would continue to supply beds in a nursing home for those women who required them.

By the start of the Second World War no progress had been made, and on 26 June 1941 the *WMN* reported that the WHF had been another casualty of the war. Not expecting to receive the same level of donations during the war, they had decided that any money on hand would be put into a savings bank and that the committee would keep the facilities available as long as funds lasted. The last annual report of the WHF was held in June 1945 and the balance in hand was donated to the Three Towns Nursing Association.

CHAPTER 5

Women in Profile: Dr Mabel Ramsay

'Dr Ramsay is a devil – we must watch her...'

Mabel Ramsay is honoured by a blue plaque at the site of her home and medical practice in North Hill. She was a doctor, a committed suffragist and an active campaigner for women's rights. In 1914 she was one of only 500 female doctors in the country.

The daughter of a naval officer, Ramsay was born in London in 1878. She determined to become a doctor early in life and qualified at the University of Edinburgh, training as a gymnast prior to her medical degree to better understand the orthopaedic work she originally planned to focus on. She qualified in 1906, eventually specialising in obstetrics and gynaecology.

In 1908 she established her medical practice in Plymouth but found resistance from the local medical establishment and, as a woman, found it difficult to secure a medical post at the city's hospitals. She applied for the post of Medical Officer of Plymouth Public Dispensary but was turned down three times, although did eventually become the consulting surgeon.

Blue Plaque on the Home and Practice of Dr Mabel Ramsay. (Chris Glasspool)

Dr Mabel Ramsay's Graduating Class, Edinburgh University (back row 2nd from left). (Edinburgh University Library under CC-BY Licence)

Plymouth Public Dispensary. (Chris Glasspool)

Also in 1908, Ramsay was asked to help form a Plymouth branch of the National Union of Women's Suffrage Societies. She subsequently became the honorary secretary and was involved in the census boycott of 1911 and women's pilgrimage to Hyde Park in 1913, along with her mother, as well as hosting and speaking at numerous meetings.

During the First World War, Dr Ramsay joined the Women's Imperial Service League and served as a doctor in Belgium under the Belgian Red Cross. She was awarded the Mons Star with Bar for service and care under fire – continuing to treat the wounded under shellfire during the allied retreat. In 1915 she joined an all-female Anglo-French team at a hospital in Cherbourg and became the hospital's Chief Medical Officer.

In 1916 she returned to Plymouth to re-establish her medical practice, secured the post of Surgeon Gynaecologist at the City Hospital and also served as a doctor at the Salisbury Road Military Hospital.

She was a founder member of the Medical Women's Federation, serving as both honorary secretary and later president and was the first female president of the Plymouth Medical Society in 1930-31. In 1921 she was only the third woman in the country to become a Fellow of the Royal College of Surgeons and was a foundation member of the Royal College of Obstetricians and Gynaecologists.

In 1929 Dr Ramsay joined with other members of the Medical Women's Federation in a letter to the *British Medical Journal* which drew attention to several appointments in the Post Office medical services being offered to women at grossly inadequate salaries and with no pension or sick pay. The writers suggested that the scale of the remuneration was an insult to the women expected to accept it and they trusted that the next government would seek to rectify this 'unjust and intolerable state of affairs'.

She was a member of many associations which worked for women's interests, including the Plymouth Citizens' Association and the Plymouth Soroptimists Club, and was involved in campaigns such as the appointment of women police officers and the establishment of a birth control clinic and continued her practice in Plymouth until 1945. She died in 1954 at a meeting of the Medical Women's Federation at the age of 75, full of drive and energy to the last. Her obituary in the *British Medical Journal* tells of her relish at recalling how it had once been said of her: 'Dr Ramsay is a devil – we must watch her.'

CHAPTER 6

Maternity and Childbirth

'Twelve children, one still-birth, four miscarriages...'

In 1915, Margaret Llewelyn Davies, General Secretary of the Women's Co-operative Guild published *Maternity: Letters from Working Women*. These poignant, moving and all too often tragic letters of women's experiences of childbirth and motherhood were collected to provide evidence of the virtually non-existent maternal and infant care available to poorer women.[1] There are stories of appalling poverty and suffering, although many are written with an astounding lack of self-pity. All end with a simple statement, such as the one quoted above, of the number of pregnancies, miscarriages and infant deaths.

Childbirth and Infant Mortality

At the turn of the nineteenth century, women married young, had their first child young and generally had large families. Miscarriage, stillbirth and infant mortality were all high and the effect of constant pregnancy on a mother's health was profound. The vast majority of women gave birth at home with no pain relief, the trusted method being to pull on a towel tied to the end of the bed when pains came.[2] While the middle and upper classes would be attended by doctors or trained midwives, working-class mothers generally could not afford such help, and instead were attended by relatives or local women. One woman recalled that her 'help' had little to offer other than the comment: 'things will get much worse yet.'[3]

Maternity homes did become available during the early twentieth century. The Three Towns Maternity Home recorded

1907	Notification of Births Act: requires medical officers of health to be informed on the birth of a child
1911	National Health Insurance Act: includes maternity benefit of 30 shillings
1915	*Maternity: Letters from Working Women* is published
1918	Maternity and Child Welfare Act: provides for establishment of local authority run ante and post-natal clinics
1921	Marie Stopes opens the first birth control clinic in London
1931	Ministry for Health issues memorandum 153/MCW which allows Maternity & Child Welfare Clinics to dispense birth control advice
1932	Mother's Advice Centre opens in Plymouth to give birth control advice
1939	*Working Class Wives*, a survey of the health of working class mothers is published
1939	Family Planning Association is formed
1961	Family planning clinics begin to prescribe the Pill
1967	Abortion Act legalises abortion in England, Wales and Scotland
1974	Family planning clinics become part of the NHS

Fig. 6.1: Timeline of Maternity and Childcare Legislation

that in the year 1924–25, there had been 177 cases admitted, twice as many as in the previous year and the home was largely used by mothers who had previously been attended in their own homes. The Alexandra Maternity Home opened in 1914 with eighteen beds and was open to wives of servicemen. But services at the maternity homes were not free and although they varied according to circumstances – the fee at the Alexandra Home ranged from twenty-one shillings to three guineas weekly – they were often beyond the range of working-class women. It was not until after the Second World War and the founding of the NHS that women began to regularly give birth in hospitals.

Unmarried mothers had few options. There were five beds at the Maternity Home in St James Terrace for unmarried mothers and St Ursula's Home took in young unmarried mothers prior to confinement and kept them for three to nine months afterwards until they could be recommended for service. Records from 1918 show that there were twenty-six births. It is unlikely that women who went into service would have been able to keep their babies, instead they may have gone to friends or family if possible, or were informally adopted. The only other option for an unmarried mother was the workhouse infirmary. In 1894 the *British Medical Journal* inspected the Plymouth workhouse as part of a campaign to improve conditions. The lying-in ward which was small and lacked privacy received particular criticism. Pregnant women slept in a ward beneath it and those waiting to give birth heard everything that went on above. When their time came they had to climb steep stairs and there were no comforts. The report described a woman who, 'by her face had experienced a hard time', sitting on a hard wooden settle and 'eating an unappetising gruel'. Attendants at workhouses tended to be pauper inmates and prior to the First World War, infant mortality rates in workhouses were more than double the rate for the rest of the population.

At the beginning of the twentieth century, concerns over the high rate of infant mortality were being raised. In February 1910, Dr Mabel Ramsay spoke on the subject in Plymouth. She maintained that more deaths were due to ignorance than any lack of love or care, and there was a need to recognise the role of fathers – she was tired of hearing how bad mothers were, yet so seldom of how bad fathers might be. She stressed the importance of education and that the school curriculum should include instruction on both motherhood and fatherhood. It was suggested to her that school was hardly the place for medical officers to discuss such intimate matters but Dr Ramsay hoped that it wasn't beyond the realms of possibility that Plymouth might one day have a female school medical officer.

The rate of infant mortality in Plymouth in 1914 was 109.7 deaths per 1,000 births compared to 105 in England and Wales as a whole. In 1918 the rates had fallen slightly to 96.6 in Plymouth and 97 for England and Wales but were still astonishingly high.

The first two decades of the twentieth century saw the first steps in creating better infant welfare services. Successive Midwives Acts ensured that midwives were trained and registered, and the 1907 Notification of Births Act required the local medical officer of health to be informed as soon as possible after a child's birth so that trained health visitors could call on the mother at home. The 1911 National Insurance Act provided for basic medical care for the working classes in return for a small payment into a compulsory insurance scheme. Pressure from the Women's Co-operative Guild ensured a maternity benefit of thirty shillings was included but otherwise wives and dependants were not covered.

Plymouth Council voluntarily adopted a scheme which established home visits for expectant mothers and infants, and post-natal clinics until the child was handed over to the Education Authority's medical services at the age of 5. In 1918 the Maternity and Child Welfare Act was passed, giving legal recognition to the child welfare services that had developed. Many towns, including Plymouth, established local-authority-run Maternity and Child Welfare clinics with access to ante-natal and post-natal services, health visitors and the provision of free milk to those in need. On 12 September 1918 the *WMN* reported that Plymouth Council would be appointing a Maternity and Child Welfare Committee which would include at least two women under the provisions of the recent Act. A social services booklet produced by Plymouth in 1920 records that there were five municipal child welfare centres under the medical officer of health, with eight health visitors and a sixth clinic held by the Three Towns Nursing Association which had its own health visitor. Medicines and dressings were supplied free to those in need and milk, food, glaxo and virol given free, or at reduced or cost price according to circumstances.

The emphasis at the beginning of the twentieth century, and particularly after the First World War, was on the importance of a woman's child-bearing role in the future health of the nation.

BETTY is now a
bonnie girl of 8 years.

BETTY at
18 months.

Betty's mother had an anxious time

Betty was prematurely born during an air-raid and weighed only 5 lbs. Within a month a narrow escape from an exploding bomb made it impossible for her mother to continue nursing her.

Betty was put on Glaxo immediately. In a few months she had grown into a bonnie Glaxo baby—a strong, happy baby.

To-day, Betty is eight years old, and a beautiful, finely proportioned girl, with no sign of "flabbiness." Glaxo has also endowed her with a vigorous constitution. Except for a simple cold she has never had a day's illness.

Mother, can you wish for better proof that Glaxo "Builds Bonnie Babies" and bonnie children too?

Glaxo

"Builds Bonnie Babies"

Over 1,500 Infant Welfare Centres have used Glaxo continuously for more than 10 years.

Advert for Glaxo at Infant Welfare Centres, 16 December 1926. (Western Morning News)

But this meant that women were targeted as the cause of infant mortality due to their maternal ignorance or lack of domestic skills. Infant mortality was even blamed on women working outside of the home. Working-class women were encouraged to strive for middle-class patterns of behaviour and to devote themselves to marriage and motherhood.[4] 'Lady visitors' would go to the homes of working-class mothers or hold 'mothers meetings' in which they gave instruction on house and mother-craft. But these endeavours, and even the initiatives of health visitors and clinics, often paid scant attention to the conditions in which working-class women lived – the poverty, the poor diet, the endless domestic chores, the necessity of work outside the home and the constant cycle of pregnancy and childbirth. Solutions to these problems were not considered, for example how a woman might safely combine employment and motherhood, or how to improve a woman's diet. Margery Spring Rice's *Working-Class Wives*, a survey published in 1939 on the health of mothers, contains numerous reports of women whose daily meals consisted of only 'bread and butter and tea'. If money was scarce then women were the first to go without and many kept such matters from their husbands, pretending that they had eaten earlier. Proposals to

Nurses with Infant Welfare Placards c.1920s. (South West Image Bank)

provide financial support to women after childbirth via National Health Insurance were put forward at the end of the First World War but rejected due to a fear that they would encourage married women to work.[5] Working-class women were presented with an ideal of motherhood which many could only fail to reach.

This is not to say that the attempts to improve infant welfare were not beneficial – while the intrusions by 'lady visitors' and even health visitors were sometimes resented, women were able to filter out information which was useful to them. Thanks to these efforts both locally and nationally the infant mortality rate did begin to drop. But the health of the mother was still all but ignored and maternal mortality rates remained high.

Maternal Mortality

On 16 July 1935 Dr Thynne of the Maternity and Child Welfare clinic, gave a lecture on maternal mortality to the Central Plymouth Townswoman's Guild. In Plymouth the number of maternal deaths was 5.93 per 1,000 live births whereas in England as a whole the figure was 4.51 per 1,000. Dr Thynne maintained that fifty per cent of these deaths were preventable. There was much that the local authorities could do to reduce the mortality rate and while Plymouth had good provision for ante and post-natal clinics and midwife training (the first in the country to offer midwife refresher training) there was still room for improvement. More health visitors were needed and maternity beds should always be provided for serious cases and those where the homes were unsuitable for confinement – in Plymouth there were still people living five or six to a room. Dr Thynne stressed the importance of women attending as many ante-natal appointments as possible and it was suggested that services needed to be more widely advertised.

Working Class Wives detailed the results of a questionnaire sent to 1,250 women by the Women's Health Enquiry Committee in response to concern over maternal health. The questionnaire asked about women's lives, families, homes and health. The responses, many of which are harrowing, highlighted the appalling conditions in which some women lived and that many suffered from a huge range of medical problems which went untreated and virtually ignored. The study confirmed that women were a class that had no easy recourse to healthcare unless they were pregnant or nursing or could afford to pay doctors' fees. Perhaps most shocking was the similarity of women's experiences in 1939 to those of the women who wrote the 'Maternity Letters' in 1915, some twenty-four years previously.

One of the issues raised by *Working Class Wives* was the toll that numerous pregnancies took on a woman. Birth control was a highly controversial subject in the early twentieth century, but improved access to birth control advice and a corresponding decline in birth rates had a great effect on women's health and maternal mortality.

CHAPTER 7

Plymouth in Profile: The Battle for Birth Control

'It is for the woman who bears the child to decide, not her husband or the state...'

In 1871 the national birth rate was 295 live births per 1,000 married women aged 15–44. By 1901 this had dropped to 222 and by the 1930s it was down to 111. Initially the decline in fertility rate was seen largely in the middle classes with working-class women continuing to have large families until at least the interwar period.[1] One of the reasons given for this was the better access the middle classes had to birth control advice via private doctors. Birth control was highly controversial, seen as immoral and unnatural and it was unlawful for doctors to pass on such information. Women either had to rely on a cooperative husband or turn to potentially dangerous methods (including gunpowder and rat poison) passed on by other women, backstreet abortionists, or 'quacks and charlatans'. Newspapers carried discreet advertisements for abortifacient pills but even these were out of reach of the average working-class woman.

In the 1920s campaigners claimed that for the good of both maternal and child health, all women should have access to such information. Radicals of the birth control movement saw Maternity and Child Welfare Clinics as the ideal place to give birth control advice, but initially the Ministry of Health resisted this notion, stating that the purpose of such clinics was to secure healthy babies, not limit their number. The Family Planning Association credits the medical officer of health for Plymouth, Dr Nankivell, as being the first to offer such clinics at Plymouth's Maternity and Child Welfare Centres in 1932.[2] Before the Plymouth case is considered however, it is worth looking at the general history of the birth control movement.

The Birth Control Movement

In 1921 the first birth control clinic was opened in London by Marie Stopes. Several more clinics followed and they eventually combined under the banner of the Family Planning Association in 1939 – but their methods were not always welcome. In 1922 a health visitor was dismissed for providing birth control advice and in 1923 Guy Aldred and his wife were prosecuted for selling a pamphlet by Margaret Sanger, an American birth control pioneer.[3] In 1926, a Bill to allow working-class women the same access to information as the middle classes was defeated in Parliament.

Later that same year, Lord Buckmaster took the issue to the House of Lords, maintaining that it was immoral to withhold details from the working classes that the middle classes already possessed. Although he talked eloquently about the horrors faced by mothers of large families living in abject poverty, he took the view that allowing the least adequate to breed so prolifically would lead to a 'deterioration of stock'. The debate is fascinating, and at times horrifying, reading. His opponents took the stand on many principles: that birth control was unnatural and immoral, against God's law and encouraging of sin; that it was dangerous to women's health and would lead to a falling birth rate; that the undeserving would be given information. The Marquess of Salisbury described women who supported the birth control movement as failing in their duty to both their husbands and the country, saying:

> We should not have pity for these lazy women or the vicious who wish to have relations but not the consequences.

A more enlightened speaker asked if women were still considered to be their husband's property and another added:

It is for the woman who bears the child to decide, not
her husband or the state.

Lord Buckmaster's motion was passed but the government
remained inactive, despite many local authorities and other
organisations sending resolutions to Parliament in favour of
giving birth control advice at welfare centres. Finally in March
1931 the Ministry of Health issued memorandum 153/MCW
which allowed welfare centres to give advice, but only where
further pregnancy would be detrimental to health. Although the
memorandum was not widely publicised, word did spread and
Margaret Pyke of the National Child Birth Association (NCBA)
persuaded several medical officers of health to run birth control
clinics on local authority premises. Plymouth was the first to do so.

Birth Control in Plymouth

In November 1931 Lady Astor wrote to Dr Nankivell regarding
the question of the high maternal mortality in Plymouth – a
rate of 6.43 deaths per 1,000 live births compared to 3.94 across
Devon as a whole. Dr Nankivell suggested that while better use
could be made of ante-natal facilities and maternity beds, much
of the mortality rate could be attributed to attempts at abortion
or the effects of previous abortion.

A dialogue with the NCBA followed regarding the setting up
of a clinic. Dr Mabel Ramsay was involved as was Dr Mildred
Thynne, the maternity officer at the Maternity and Child
Welfare Clinic at Beaumont Park who was described as very
sympathetic and doing what she could unofficially for mothers.

On 2 May 1932, the *WMN* recorded that the Plymouth
Maternity and Child Welfare Committee had given permission,
subject to the approval by the Ministry of Health, for the NCBA
to use the welfare centre at Beaumont Park as a birth control clinic.

In correspondence between Lady Astor and the NCBA
there was much discussion over the delicacy of the subject.
Terms such as birth control, contraception and abortion were
considered too controversial and it was agreed that the clinic

should be called a Mother's Advice Centre. The clinic would give sound and serious information to working mothers, would be run by a qualified woman doctor and nurses, and would not disseminate knowledge unsuitable or morally dangerous to its recipients. Birth control was seen as a measure to improve a woman's health and lead to healthier and better planned families rather than giving women the right to control their own fertility.[4] A meeting to discuss the clinic was planned but it was agreed not to advertise too widely to prevent undesirables attending. Despite their caution, the *WMN* of 7 May 1932 reported that a large emergency meeting of Roman Catholic clergy and laymen had been held at Devonport where they protested the 'insidious evil' of the proposal. A resolution was unanimously passed that:

> Bearing in mind the immoral character and the evil effects of the practice of artificial birth prevention, we protest emphatically against the proposed birth control clinic … as ratepayers we urge upon the council to veto these proposals.

Birth control was considered contrary to the laws of the church and against nature and they were looking at the subject for the good of the British Nation which:

> If it continued in this practice would fall like the Roman Empire.

But despite this protest, on 25 June 1932 the Ministry of Health confirmed it had no objections to the clinic. It did however caution that should the birth control clinic be in any way detrimental to the work of the Maternity and Child Welfare Centre then it would be closed at short notice.

Lady Astor was invited to be president of the Plymouth Birth Control Association but although she declined this she did fully support it and contributed significantly to funding. On 28 September 1932, the Women's Co-operative Guild met in advance of the opening of the Mother's Advice Centre. Mrs Godfrey Bird, secretary of the new clinic and Mrs Mattison, the treasurer, confirmed that the introduction of the clinic would in no way stamp out the maternal instinct. Apart from a small fee charged, the clinic would be funded by voluntary donations and run by Dr Norah Goodbody supported by a trained nurse. In October it was confirmed that the cost of running the clinic would be about £150 per year and although around 700 appeals had been sent out, only £12 had been raised. Lady Astor stepped in to ensure funding for the first year but funding continued to be an issue as did the difficulty of reaching the very poor, who were perhaps most in need of advice. By 1939 the clinic had been granted a lump sum by the City Council, but in April 1940 it was reported the clinic ran twice a month rather than weekly due to financial strain. Plymouth was at least one of the few towns getting municipal support however.

Despite the financial issues, the clinics continued and by the 1950s they began to give pre-marital advice to women. The 1960s saw the introduction of the Pill and in 1974 clinics were handed over to the NHS and family planning became a part of the health service.

Despite much opposition to them, the early birth control clinics played an important part in breaking the cycle of constant childbearing. Publications such as *Working Class Wives* and *Maternity: Letters From Working Women* show that many women were entirely ignorant of birth control and would have welcomed any advice were it available. Perhaps the final word should be left to a woman who wrote to the *WMN* in 1932, when a birth control clinic was still being debated. The anonymous writer was married with six children and the family of eight lived in one room. She wrote:

> Mother-love amongst the working classes is simply wonderful. It is the same mother-love that is rousing mothers of large families to think about the children they have now and to do what they think best for them. When women fight they fight to win. From one who has six children and is young enough to have six more.

CHAPTER 8

Marriage and the Home

'My wife she is a bonny lass,
None more free from evil.
Except 'tis on a washing day
And then she is a devil!'

Marriage, Divorce and Custody of Children

In the nineteenth century, a woman's expected role was that of wife and mother. If a marriage was sound then all was well, but if not then circumstances for women could be very difficult. Until the late nineteenth century a married woman had few legal rights. The policy of coverture meant that on marriage a woman legally ceased to be a person in her own right and became subsumed by her husband. All property and wealth she possessed prior to marriage, or that she earned or inherited during the marriage, passed to him and she was unable to make contracts in her own name. This particular inequality was one of the issues that helped encourage the feminist movements of the mid-nineteenth century, but it wasn't until 1870 that the Married Woman's Property Act gave a woman possession of money and investments she earned after marriage. A further Act of 1882 allowed women to retain ownership of property and wealth held prior to marriage and a third Act of 1893 effectively ended the policy of coverture.

The laws over property were of more concern to the middle classes, but divorce and custody of children was an issue for all women. In the early nineteenth century, divorce was impossible for all but the most privileged woman and prior to 1839, a woman had no rights over the custody of her children. The

1839	Custody of Children Act: women can petition for custody of children under 7
1857	Divorce and Matrimonial Causes Act: allows divorce through adultery
1870	Married Women's Property Act: women retain earnings after marriage
1873	Infant Custody Act: women can petition for custody of children under 16
1878	Matrimonial Causes Act: women can obtain a judicial separation
1882	Married Women's Property Act: women retain property after marriage
1891	Guardianship and Custody of Children Act
1893	Married Women's Property Act: policy of coverture ends
1908	Children's Act: provides further protection for children
1923	Matrimonial Causes Act: women have equal right to petition for divorce
1969	Divorce Reform Act
1976	Domestic Violence and Matrimonial Proceedings Act
1994	Rape in marriage made a crime
2004	Domestic Violence Crime & Victims Act: overhauls domestic violence laws

Fig. 8.1: Timeline of Marriage and Custody of Children Legislation

1839 Custody of Infants Act allowed a mother to petition the courts for custody of children up to the age of 7, and for access in respect of older children, after a sustained campaign by Caroline Norton. Having left her abusive husband, Norton had been denied access to their children, and one of her sons died following a riding accident before she was able to reach him. A further Infant Custody Act of 1873 changed the emphasis to the needs of the child and allowed women to petition for custody of children under 16.

The 1857 Divorce and Matrimonial Causes Act allowed divorce to be obtained through the courts on the grounds of proven adultery. For men, one transgression from their wife was enough for divorce to be granted. Women had not only to prove adultery, but also an aggravating factor such as cruelty, neglect, bigamy or incest. Divorce proceedings were held in open court and high costs meant they remained the province of the middle and upper classes – legal aid did not become freely available until 1946.[1] The working classes were more likely to make use of informal separation and the 1878 Matrimonial Causes Act allowed women who were the victims of violence in marriage to obtain a judicial separation order from a magistrate.

Domestic abuse was unfortunately a fact of life for some women. Although abhorrent to many, there was an underlying belief that as a man's wife and children were considered to be his property, he could physically discipline them, and women were perhaps more willing to endure occasional violence against them when their alternatives were poverty or the workhouse. The *WMN* of 8 May 1860 reported on a parliamentary debate over a Bill permitting magistrates to sanction corporal punishment to husbands guilty of brutality. One opponent of the Bill suggested some men could be provoked into violence by 'an angry woman's tongue', and the newspaper went on to describe the 'peculiar powers of aggravation which women possess', and how they 'will irritate and vex, all uttered with the most innocent air'. The conclusion was that:

> Surely if cases of brutal assaults by husbands are so frequent, it is the woman's tongue that is to blame.

This was too much for one lady reader from the Three Towns. In a reply to the newspaper she wrote:

> I hope for the sake of common humanity, that the article was not intended as a justification for domestic violence.... Men forget that their tongues possess the same weapons and conveniently ignore the amount of

cursing and swearing bestowed on some poor women. The example given of a drunken husband coming home to a shrill and complaining wife neglects to mention the all too common situation of the wife waiting for her husband to bring home wages so that she might buy food for herself and her children only to find that it has already been spent on drink and debauchery. It is understandable that she might express her reproach, but does she then deserve a beating for it? As a poor woman with nothing but my tongue I cannot venture an opinion as to what remedy might stop such evil. I apologise for intruding but since I have done so by pen instead of tongue I do not stand in dread of a thrashing.

The outcome of judicial separation hearings depended on the views of the magistrates who at times would try to reconcile husband and wife. On 5 August 1880 the *WMN* reported from the Devonport Petty Sessions. A dockyard labourer had been summoned for an unlawful assault on his wife. He had been summoned for assault twelve months previously but on the recommendation of the bench the matter was compromised and the wife went back to live with him. However, his behaviour grew worse until he threatened her with a knife. The wife gave evidence that her husband was vicious and spent the greater part of his wages to the neglect of his home and witnesses testified to his dangerous character. The bench made an order for a judicial separation and a payment of five shillings per week for maintenance.

Following the First World War there was reform to the divorce laws, particularly with regard to women. The 1923 Matrimonial Causes Act allowed women to petition for divorce on the same grounds as men, and in 1937 the Act was amended to include cruelty, desertion and incurable insanity as grounds for divorce. On 28 June 1938 the *WMN* announced that divorce petitions under the new Act had been held for the first time in Plymouth. Thirty-four suits had been dealt with and all had been given a decree nisi. Reasons for divorce included desertion, not making a suitable home, a wife's overspending on beauty treatments, cruelty and drunkenness.

Divorce was still uncommon through the first half of the twentieth century but the Divorce Reform Act of 1969 perhaps combined with a change in attitudes and the growing economic independence of women to increase the divorce rate.

Housing

The Three Towns were notorious for overcrowding, exacerbated by the growth of the dockyard. Initially workers had been housed in hulks, but although petitioning for housing did lead to some provision, many lived in little more than slums and census returns give details of the overcrowding. In 1841, Elizabeth Beer, daughter of a stonemason, lived with her parents, siblings and two other families in a house in Waterloo Street. A total of sixteen people resided in the one property – six adults and ten children. The census of 1851 shows that on average there were more than two families, or more than ten people, to a house. The average across the rest of the country was five people per house. One of the worst areas of overcrowding was around the Barbican, with Castle Dyke Lane averaging twenty-four people per house. The King Street area, near Union Street, had 825 people living in sixty-seven houses, fifty-seven of which had no water.

Ill-health and epidemics were rife; a cholera outbreak in 1849 caused the deaths of 1,894 people in the Three Towns and in 1872 a smallpox outbreak killed 448.

Slum housing had an appalling lack of facilities; many houses had no water supply, rooms were crowded with beds, cooking was done on open fires and the attempt to keep the property clean was a constant battle for housewives. In December 1846 Plymouth Town Council adopted an Act which encouraged the establishment of public baths and washhouses for the working classes. Although there is some evidence that communal facilities were unpopular with women, who valued their privacy,[2] the washhouse in Plymouth seems to have been

Housing in Looe Street, Plymouth c.1920s. (South West Image Bank)

well used. Wash-day at home was generally considered to be the worst day of the week and many men preferred to spend the evening at the pub rather than return home. The *Western Courier* of 4 September 1850 reported that since its opening in January, the wash-house at Hoegate Street had proved most popular, with an estimated 5,100 people washing and drying their laundry. A letter to the editor of the *Western Courier* in April 1851 bemoans the lack of a washhouse in Devonport particularly in the area of Dockwall street where:

> Masses of human beings are heaped together, three or four families living in a room scarcely sufficient for one … some of the women take in washing which has to be dried indoors.

The writer ends his letter with the poem quoted at the start of the chapter.

In 1874 the closure of the wash-houses was considered as they were costing the town over £100 per year to run, but it was agreed that the benefit to the women outweighed the

---

PLYMOUTH PUBLIC BATHS AND WASH-HOUSES, HOEGATE-STREET. WM. ROWE having become the Lessee of the above Establishment, begs respectfully to announce that he has thoroughly cleansed and renovated every department, and made such additions and improvements as appeared to him to be conducive to the comfort and convenience of the public, together with a judicious selection of persons to whom the superintendence and management will be entrusted. He therefore respectfully solicits a visit from his friends, and from persons to whom the advantages and moderate charges of this establishment are not well known. He also confidently hopes for the continued support and patronage of those Ladies and Gentlemen who have been accustomed to use those Baths.

SCALE OF PRICES.

LADIES.	Hot or Cold.	s.	d.	GENTLEMEN.	Hot or Cold.	s.	d.
Bath Rooms		1	0	Bath Rooms		1	0
1st Class Bath		0	6	1st Class Bath		0	6
2nd do. do.		0	4	2nd do. do.		0	4
3rd do. do.		0	3	3rd do. do.		0	3

Second Class Cold, 2d. ; Third, 1½d.
Plunge, Douche, and Shower Baths.
Each Bather is supplied with clean Towels.

WASHING DEPARTMENT.

1st Class compartment, 1½d. per hour; 2nd do., 1d. ; with the use of Hot Air Drying Room.

W. R. begs to state that the Bathing and Washing Departments, although parts of one establishment, are entirely distinct, having separate entrances, with separate waiting-rooms for Ladies and Gentlemen.

Resident Superintendent, Mr. Wm. HILL.
Matron, Mrs. HILL.
Engineer, Mr. J. PURDIE.
Ladies' Bath Attendant Mrs. PURDIE.
Lessee, Mr. Wm. ROWE, Tavistock-street.

Advert for Plymouth Public Washhouse, 24 September 1861. (Western Morning News)

cost. In 1885, 200 women who used them were treated to a tea and entertainment and they survived well into the twentieth century.

The 1890 Housing of the Working Class Act compelled local authorities to act on the problems of slum housing and in response Plymouth Council established a Housing Committee. The first council houses were built in Laira Bridge Road in 1896, partly to re-house people displaced by slum clearance, but the Three Towns entered the twentieth century with continued overcrowding. The 1901 census shows that average occupation was still more than eight people per house, with many accommodated in just one room, and the 1921 census indicated that in Plymouth only twenty-seven per cent of families were in individual dwellings.

Writing in 1900 H. F. Whitefield described the uncared-for streets of Plymouth with 'children who border on a state of nudity and with men and women not much better clothed'. Even by the 1930s, social surveys showed that overcrowding in Plymouth was worse than in East London and Liverpool and that sixteen per cent of families were living below the poverty line.[3]

The Three Towns did embark on a programme of slum clearance but financial considerations meant progress was slow. In the *WMN* on 28 June 1930 Rev. Allwork of St Georges, Stonehouse said:

> The continued existence of areas which were scheduled for demolition four years ago should make Plymouth hang its head in shame. Repairing the properties was a waste of money and the unfortunate tenants of these germ-infested dwellings were paying the price for their poverty.

In 1933 a five-year plan was announced. Details of the areas to be targeted show the conditions in which people were still living. Seventeen houses in Moon and North Street were to be demolished, displacing 206 people, which meant an average occupation of twelve people per house. In March 1934 the Mayoress spoke at an American tea organised by a committee of women who wanted to add to the funds of Plymouth Housing Improvement Society. The Mayoress commended the society on their voluntary efforts to help towards the clearing of slums, especially with a view to helping the very poorest who could not afford any but the lowest rents. As women they were all house-proud and recognised that so too were the housewives of the slums.

The Second World War slowed slum clearance, but the war was to have a more drastic effect. The devastating Plymouth Blitz flattened much of the city leaving thousands homeless, but out of the destruction came Patrick Abercrombie and James Paton Watson's 'Plan for Plymouth'; a vision that allowed for planning and rebuilding of the city on a huge scale. Both the terrible effects of the Blitz and the old overcrowded housing would be replaced with a new and modern Plymouth which worked for all its occupants.

In May 1944 Lady Astor addressed the first annual meeting of the Standing Conference of Women's Organisations. She said that women needed to cooperate in order to see through the new Plymouth Plan. It was estimated that 20,000 houses would be needed in the ten years to 1955 to replace both blitzed and slum properties and to account for pre-war shortage. New housing estates were built, spilling into the surrounding countryside and Plymouth extended its boundaries further. By 1956, 14,374 council houses and 2,283 private houses had been built, and by 1964 Plymouth had passed the 20,000 target.[4]

Labour-Saving Devices

The gradual introduction of gas, electricity and labour-saving devices to the home transformed women's daily lives. Although cooking and washing still needed to be done, the time saved by the use of gas and electric ovens, washing machines and refrigerators meant more opportunity for work outside the home or leisure.

Gas: In the early nineteenth century, the most common use of gas was in street lighting and the first General Meeting of the Plymouth and Stonehouse Gas Light and Coke Co. was held at Plymouth Guildhall on 30 July 1845.

With competition from electricity however, gas companies eventually began to diversify into cooking and heating towards the end of the century. In 1893 an exhibition of gas appliances, including cookers, coffee roasters and washing machines, was held at St Andrew's Hall in Plymouth, where a cookery demonstration was given to

Advert for Gas Cooker, 5 October 1938. (Western Morning News)

around 200 women. The Gas Light and Coke Co. also installed a model flat in their showrooms at 26 George Street, fitted with labour-saving devices. Lights were controlled by switches, water heaters gave instantaneous hot water, the dining room and bedrooms had gas fires and the kitchen contained a gas washing machine, refrigerator and an enamelled cooker which required only seven minutes to heat to a temperature suitable for roasting.

Electricity: In September 1899 the Mayor of Plymouth opened the Plymouth Corporation Electricity Works at Prince Rock and the first electric trams were inaugurated, but it would be another two years before Devonport and Stonehouse had a public electricity supply. Initially the supply was used for the trams, limited street lighting and some minor private use; the connection of houses to the supply did not really take off until the 1930s and was then used mainly for lighting. In 1933 it was reported that the supply of electricity to the working classes was being tackled as slums were cleared and new houses appeared. The Electrical Association for Women (EAW) was formed in 1926 with the aim of promoting the wider use of electricity in the service of women. The founder was Mrs M. L. Matthews, a member of the Women's Engineering Society, and she was clear that electricity in the home would revolutionise housework and was the 'hope of the housewife'.[5] A Plymouth & District branch

CITY OF PLYMOUTH
ELECTRICITY
DEPARTMENT

new showrooms
83 Old Town Street
telephone 2821

Scientific Displays of Shop Window Lighting
Full Range of Cookers for Hire
Cleaners, Fires, Water Heaters, Refrigerators
and all types of Domestic Appliances

SEE FOR YOURSELVES
WHAT
ELECTRICITY WILL DO

Advert for Electricity Showrooms, Plymouth, 6 June 1936. (Western Morning News)

of the association was formed which held meetings and lectures and paid visits to local institutions such as the Prince Rock Power Station. In December 1929 an exhibition of electrical goods for Christmas was given to demonstrate 'numerous electrical home apparatus, both useful and decorative'. In March 1932, Miss Bullwistle gave a lecture and practical demonstration on cooking with electricity. She said that:

> One of the advantages of an electric oven was that if used correctly the dinner could be put on and then one could go out shopping with no fear of it burning – a real boon for the busy housewife.

In October 1933 at a meeting in Plymouth of the Devon and Cornwall Counties Federation of the Electrical Association of Women, the view of electricity as a 'servant' of women was stressed. Electric lighting prevented accidents caused by badly lit stairs and passages and cleared the smoky atmosphere which was so bad for health. Careers for women as demonstrators of electrical appliances were also discussed, with lectures being organised at the association headquarters in London for those interested. In June 1936 the Plymouth Corporation Electricity Department opened new showrooms at 83 Old Town Street, including a demonstration theatre with cookers and a refrigerator and the EAW was provided with refreshments cooked and prepared on the site. The initial cost of apparatus however was still too great for 'ordinary people' and it was stressed that only when manufacturers could find the means of reducing the cost would the working-classes enjoy the full benefits. An 'all electric' house was established on the Tor Meadow Estate which incorporated:

> All those features which had done so much to lighten the load of the modern housewife and to solve the problems created by the domestic servant shortage. Washing and boiling machines eliminated the drudgery of laundry and water heaters gave a constant supply of hot water. The

kitchen had a refrigerator and cooker and all lighting and heating was electric, including a coal-effect fire to give a warming glow. The bathroom had a heated airing cupboard and even the garage had a car-heating device.

In June 1937 the *Western Morning News* reported on the benefits of a refrigerator, which allowed food to be bought in bulk and stored safely for longer, cutting down on the time and cost spent on shopping. Mrs Lindsey Davies would give a demonstration of cold cookery at the electrical showrooms and one recipe was as follows:

Cherry Moss: Soak 1 tbsp gelatine in 2 tbsps cold water and then dissolve in one teacup of hot water. Add one cup canned cherries (stoned and halved) and one cup cherry juice. When mixture thickens, mix in two stiffly beaten egg-whites. Put into an oiled mould and chill. Unmould and decorate with whipped cream and chopped pistachio nuts.

The introduction of labour-saving devices did not of course affect all women equally and it was the middle-classes who benefited initially. By the end of the First World War, working-class groups such as the Women's Labour League were making three basic demands in new housing design – an indoor bathroom, a scullery/kitchen and a front parlour. But for many women living in rooms and slums with no access to a kitchen, cooking on an open-fire remained the only option until well into the inter-war period; even where electricity and gas was supplied it was often only used for lighting and heating. By 1949 across the country, seventy-nine per cent of homes had a gas supply, eight-six per cent had electricity and sixty-eight per cent had both, yet only nineteen per cent of homes had an electric cooker, fifteen per cent a water heater, four per cent a washing machine and two per cent a fridge.[6] It wasn't until some years after the Second World War that the use of gas and electricity in the home really began to benefit the working-class wife.

SPOONERS

Specialists in Refrigerators

To you, Coldspot means new appreciation of food — vegetables coming to the table as if just from your own garden ! For you Coldspot means new health — milk and meat *safe !* To you Coldspot means new household economy — food kept cheaply, food that was dearly thrown away before. *Just a few of the things that*

Coldspot does for better living. Coldspot brings you new, better entertaining — delighting your guests with fresh, enticing dishes. Coldspot gives you best-value-ever in refrigeration — new planning for more space, new labour-saving devices, new lowest-ever prices. Coldspot adds new beauty to your kitchen — lovely, last word designs in gleaming white and chromium. You can rely on Coldspot — fully guaranteed — born of the vast refrigerator experience of Sears Roebuck — the world's largest merchandising organization.

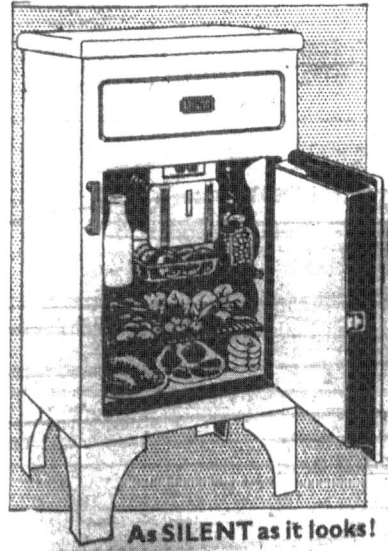

3·85 CUBIC FEET

28 GNS.

SPECIAL THREE

Height 44½" Width 24½"
Depth 24½"   3 Shelves
64 Ice Cubes (5 lbs.)
9 stages of coldness

or 30/- deposit   No Interference with
15/- monthly   wireless sets !

FIVE YEARS GUARANTEE AND FREE SERVICE — FOUR YEARS TO PAY

Look for these Coldspot features !
(ALL MODELS) *Touch-a-Bar Door Opener, Automatic Interior Light, Rustless Shelves, Perfect Insulation, Beautiful Enamel Finish, 9-Point Cold Control.*

As SILENT as it looks!

Coldspot ELECTRIC REFRIGERATORS

PRODUCTS OF SEARS ROEBUCK

SPOONER & COMPANY LIMITED, PLYMOUTH. Phone 2814

Advert for Spooners Refrigerators, 21 June 1937. (Western Morning News)

CHAPTER 9

Poverty and Philanthropy

'We are no ordinary women...'

Poverty and the Workhouse

Poverty was an unfortunate fact of life for many residents of the Three Towns and the workhouse an ever-present threat. Life in the workhouse was gruelling and for many it was the last resort after all else had failed. Figure 9.1 shows the occupation of the workhouse from census records and indicates that in general the female population was slightly higher than the male, particularly in Devonport and Stonehouse.

In 1832, a Royal Commission reviewed the haphazard poor law system and the result was the 1834 Poor Law Amendment Act which imposed a new standard across the country. Parishes were grouped together to operate large workhouses and Poor Law Unions were created to administer poor relief, governed by a Board of Guardians who controlled finances and administration. Funding came from the local poor rate paid by all ratepayers. The Act took a far harsher view of poverty, declaring it to be caused by individuals rather than social or economic conditions. The 'workhouse test' was revived which meant that workhouse conditions should be so repellent that anyone prepared to accept such relief must be lacking in the moral determination to survive outside it. Able-bodied inmates were required to work, often hard, monotonous activities such as 'oakum-picking', whereby old ropes were unpicked into fibres to be sold to the navy or ship builders. With its maritime setting this was a common occupation in the Three Towns' workhouses. Another controversial part of the Act was that illegitimate children were made the sole responsibility of the mother until they were 16. If a woman was unable to support herself and her children they would all need to enter the workhouse. This was overturned in 1844 and mothers were given the possibility of claiming maintenance from the father of the child, but in reality this rarely happened.

Figures 9.2 and 9.3 give more detail of the female occupants of Devonport workhouse taken from the 1881 census.[1] The vast majority of women were unmarried or widowed and of those who were married, only one was in the workhouse with her husband. Although only conjecture, it is easy enough to imagine the circumstances which led these women to such a situation, especially those with young children: Louisa Eddy, an unmarried dressmaker with her infant daughter, Bessie Netherway, an unmarried charwoman with a 3-year-old son, and Catherine Herring, an unmarried domestic servant of just 19 with her baby son, Herbert. These single women were not eligible to claim the outdoor relief available to their married sisters, and often their only option for a place to give birth was the workhouse infirmary. Even married women sometimes could not avoid the workhouse – Mary Jane O'Brien was an inmate with her five children aged from 10 months to 12 years. There were seventy-eight widows, including Sara Slaney and her four children, and fifty-two of the widowed women were over 60. There were also fifty children under the age of 15 in the workhouse, and many of these were either orphaned or abandoned, like John Garside, aged 6, and sisters Eliza and Jessie Grant aged 6 and 2. The view of the 1832 Royal Commission that those in poverty had no one to blame but themselves seems particularly ruthless when the individual circumstances of inmates are examined like this, in an age of no pensions or sickness benefits, in which women were discouraged from working and unmarried mothers were vilified.

By the end of the nineteenth century however, change was in the wind. Boards of Guardians had traditionally been dominated by wealthy, property-owning men, but two factors changed this dynamic. Firstly there was the election of significant numbers

| | Plymouth | | Devonport | | Stonehouse | |
	Male	Female	Male	Female	Male	Female
1861	210	242	165	251	23	50
1871	274	274	190	248	38	56
1881	304	315	137	214	33	56
1891	275	290	134	174	26	35
1901	382	279	129	188	32	50
1911	247	285	71	121	24	47

Fig. 9.1: Inmates of the Three Towns Workhouses from Census Data

of female guardians and secondly, in 1892, the property rental value qualifying a person for election was lowered, allowing more working-class people to stand. This meant a diversification of Board members and they began to draw attention to the many failings of the system. In December 1905 a commission on the Poor Law and Unemployed was appointed and spent four years preparing a report. The commission was split in its views but, although in a minority, there was a call for the complete abolishment of the Poor Laws. Perhaps because of the scale of the reform required, no new legislation followed until after the First World War, but in 1925 the Health Minister, Neville Chamberlain, began to look at altering the system. The 1929 Local Government Act brought about many of the measures proposed by the 1909 report and Boards of Guardians were abolished; their responsibilities transferred to local authorities.

Age	No. Women	Unmarried	Married	Widowed
15-21	9	3	0	0
21-60	89	54	9	26
Over 60	77	19	5	52
Total[a]	175	76	14	78

[a]Marital status not recorded for all 175 women over 15

Fig. 9.2: Age & Marital Status of Devonport Workhouse Female Inmates from 1881 Census

Occupation	No. Women	Occupation	No. Women
Charwomen	34	Shopkeeper	1
Domestic Servant	31	Straw Bonnet Maker	1
Tailoress/Needlewomen	17	Butt Woman	1
Fruit seller/Dealer	4	Naval Engineer's Wife	1
Laundress	4	Prostitute	1
Fishwoman	2	No Recorded Occupation	54
Boot Closer	1	Lunatic/Imbecile/Idiot	23

Fig. 9.3: Previous Occupations of Devonport Workhouse Female Inmates from 1881 Census

Although progress was slow, physical conditions did at last improve for the inmates who continued to be mainly the elderly, those with mental health problems, unmarried mothers and vagrants. The National Health Service Act of 1946 brought further changes and institutions came under the control of Hospital Management Committees, although many still carried the old workhouse stigma and some maintained Reception Centres for Wayfarers (i.e. casual wards for vagrants) until as late as the 1960s.

Philanthropists

There were those who fought to improve the lives of the working classes and the Three Towns were not lacking in this respect. Rescue homes worked to reclaim prostitutes and find them alternative work, scattered homes were an alternative to the workhouse for orphaned and abandoned children, and churches and charities collected and fundraised for many causes.

In 1848 the Bishop of Exeter, Henry Phillpotts, issued an appeal to the 'Christian charity of England' for assistance in the areas of Devonport and Plymouth which urgently needed help, churches and schools. Priscilla Lydia Sellon, 27-year-old daughter of Commander Richard Baker Smith of the Royal Navy, was bound for Italy for her health when she heard of the appeal and, abandoning her voyage, she answered the call. She settled in Morice Town, one of the most destitute districts, and was introduced to the Reverend Killpack of St James. With a companion, Miss Chambers, she rented rooms in George Street and adopted the clothes and manners of her neighbours so as to win confidence. She came into contact with the children who:

> Swarmed the streets in a neighbourhood described as the haunt of every vice and misery ... whose evils were not even veiled.[2]

Initially working in an existing but poorly run school she and her companion soon founded new establishments including an industrial school for girls, an evening school for boys, a school for the starving and the Home for Orphan Daughters of British Sailors and Soldiers. Inspired by Bishop Phillpotts, she formed an Anglican Sisterhood who worked for the good of the community. Their official title was the Church of England Sisterhood of Mercy of Devonport and Plymouth. The women showed scant regard for Victorian proprieties of the day, often walking the streets after dark when ministering to the sick, and during the cholera epidemic of 1849 the Sisters worked tirelessly, day and night. When they first approached the vicar of the parish most affected by the illness he was:

> At first inclined out of kindness to refuse their services. It seemed unthinkable that English ladies should be asked to deal at close grips with this horror.[3]

But Miss Sellon was not easily turned from such work. 'We are no ordinary women', she told the vicar.

There was considerable conflict with the protestant religion in Plymouth who disliked the Church of Rome connotations of the Sisterhood, even to the point (as the Sisterhood saw it) of opening rival Orphan Asylums to try to attract girls away. The vicar of St Andrews was particularly negative and, with two newspapers and a lawyer on his side, ran a sustained campaign to try to force closure of the Sisterhood. He had support from clergy from elsewhere in the country and newspaper reports and pamphlets detailed the 'sinister' religious practices of the Sisterhood. There also seemed to be a particular anxiety over many of the 'genteel' female members of the Sisterhood having to do 'menial tasks and domestic work'. The Reverend William Colles, said:

> God forbid we should stop the flow of Christian charity;
> but we must protest against the system of drawing young
> ladies away from their homes.[4]

Lydia Sellon and her supporters countered all the attacks and abuse and despite her own failing health and eventual paralysis she saw her Sisterhood spread throughout the country and open its first purpose-built convent, Ascot Priory, in Berkshire. She died in 1876 at the age of 55.

Perhaps the most well-known female philanthropist of Plymouth was Dame Agnes Weston, the subject of the next chapter, whose legacy continues today.

CHAPTER 10

Women in Profile: Dame Agnes Weston

'The sailor's friend...'

Agnes Weston was born in London in 1840, the daughter of a barrister. A philanthropist involved in social welfare and a temperance activist, she is best remembered as 'the sailor's friend' after her pioneering work in Plymouth and Portsmouth. She was the first woman to be buried with full Naval honours.

In April 1868 Weston began to correspond with sailor George Brown, and she was soon receiving letters from many other sailors. She began to write a *Monthly Letter* and a magazine *Ashore and Afloat* for distribution on British Navy ships and as a member of the National Temperance League she sought a way to divert sailors from the temptations of inns and brothels.

In 1873 she came to Devonport to meet some of the sailors who were coming into port. Sophie Wintz, who would become her lifelong friend and partner, invited her to address a meeting of sailors' wives and it was at the Wintz family home that their work began. They opened up the kitchen to sailors as a welcoming place for a cup of coffee and a chat. This proved so popular that a deputation from HMS *Dryad* asked her to open a temperance house near the dockyard gates and Weston progressed to providing facilities with overnight accommodation. The first of these houses was opened at Fore Street in Devonport on 8 May 1876 and was followed by others in Portsmouth and Gosport. The houses were known as 'Sailor's Rests' and, as an alternative to public houses, they provided a safe 'home from home' where a sailor could find a cheap meal, a bed and a friendly ear if needed – many young men found them a lifeline. In her autobiography *My Life Among the Bluejackets,* Agnes Weston remembers the anger of the local publicans who described the Rests as 'a disgraceful innovation' and questioned whether Agnes and Sophie could be called 'ladies' due to their work.[1] In response, Agnes and Sophie started a scheme to raise enough money to buy out the public houses around Fore Street and donations flowed in from all places, including the sailors themselves. One young man brought a sovereign from his fiancée who was in service and when asked why she took such interest he replied – 'because of the change she sees in me'. Eventually the inns were bought and demolished and the Sailor's Rest expanded.

Dame Weston took a keen interest in the welfare of sailors' wives and families and they were always welcomed at the Rests. Club days were held with crèches for the children, stalls sold materials and clothing, and a library and temperance society were established for the women. A committee of sailors' wives organised bazaars to raise money, a portion of which was given to the Victoria Jubilee Nurses who were available for maternity and district nursing. They also ran a maternity club where members were encouraged to save at least £1. The mothers were then given a percentage on top of the money saved to be used for a skilled nurse, groceries and little comforts.

Dame Weston was also involved in the reform of payments of half-pay wages to sailors' wives. Half-pay was paid on a certain date at the pay office at the dockyard and the women had to receive it personally. This could mean a walk of several miles no matter what the weather, often with children in tow. The conditions were sometimes so bad that women would faint in the waiting room or become ill, and if a woman should arrive too late for her payment the entire journey would need to be repeated on 'recall' day. This old, outdated system was brought to the attention of the Admiralty and Parliament by Mr Kearley MP, and both Weston and Wintz helped in interviewing witnesses and gathering and giving evidence.

As a result the system was overhauled so that a woman receiving half-pay would get a postal order each month that could be cashed when needed at her nearest post office.

Dame Weston administered an emergency fund for the help of women whose sons and husbands were lost at sea.

Dame Agnes Weston. (Aggies.co.uk)

The immediate effect on the death of a sailor was a cessation of pay which could lead to poverty and even starvation for his dependants. Those who were registered on half-pay and whose husband or son died on active service received a Greenwich Pension for wives and children and a gratuity payment for mothers. However, some sailors were not registered, simply sending home what money they could spare. The wives of these sailors were not on Admiralty books and if they could not prove that they received regular payments from their husbands they would receive no pension. Weston recalled one case where a woman whose husband had drowned and whose rent was in arrears was threatened by bailiffs just days after her husband's death. Through the emergency fund they were able to save her home. In 1893, following the loss of **HMS** *Victoria* in the Mediterranean, Dame Weston was instrumental in starting an appeal to help the families of those who had lost their lives until Admiralty or other assistance came into effect. Such payments

Royal Sailors Rest, Fore Street, Devonport. (Aggies.co.uk)

continued until official help was available and Weston admitted that she often cleared out every penny she had and then would begin the fundraising over again.

In 1892 Queen Victoria bestowed the title 'Royal' on the Sailor's Rests and in 1893 Agnes was invited to Windsor to meet her. In 1918 Agnes was made a Dame of the British Empire and died on 23 October 1918 in her Sailor's Rest in Devonport. Her funeral took place in the church at the dockyard and she was buried with full naval honours. Two thousand sailors were present as well as representatives from the Royal Marines, Army, RAF, WRNS and the American Navy. Bluejackets lined the road from the Sailor's Rest to the church and the coffin was transported on a gun carriage, covered by the Union Jack and drawn by sailors with two admirals following on foot.[2] The coffin was interred at Weston Mill Cemetery and her memorial stone proclaims her: 'The Sailor's Friend'. Sophie Wintz carried on the work until she died in 1929. She was also given a full naval funeral and was buried with Agnes Weston. Their work continues today in the form of 'Aggies' – an organisation which provides help and pastoral support to members of the Royal Navy, the Royal Marines and their families. One project run by Aggies is Storybook Waves which keeps families connected by allowing anyone serving away from home to record bedtime stories for their children.[3]

CHAPTER 11

Votes For Women

'A woman's point of view is just as worthy of consideration...'

On 29 March 1870, at a meeting at the Mechanics' Institute, Plymouth, a resolution to present a memorial to Parliament in favour of the franchise for women was unanimously carried. The principal speakers at the meeting were women's suffrage supporters Walter Morrison MP and William Collier, who moved that:

> It is unwise and unjust that the suffrage for the election
> of members of Parliament should be limited to one sex
> and that it is expedient to admit women to the franchise.

The Rise of the Suffrage Campaign

The campaign for votes for women was most vocal during the late nineteenth and early twentieth century, but calls for enfranchisement were made much earlier. In 1832, Henry Hunt MP presented a petition from Mary Smith of Yorkshire requesting the parliamentary vote on the basis that she paid taxes and was subject to the law in the same way as qualified men. The petition was dismissed but apparently caused much amusement in the House of Commons. Miss Smith had been moved to action by the 1832 Representation of the People Act which had expressly excluded women from the franchise by the inclusion of the term 'male person'. The Act also triggered the rise of Chartism, a working-class movement which pressed for the vote for all men over the age of 21 and, in its early stages, included women's suffrage. Although Chartism ended by the

1850s without achieving its aims, the issue of electoral reform had been raised in the public eye.

By the mid 1860s there was the promise of a second electoral reform bill and a burgeoning feminist movement which had begun to question the limitations faced by women. From the Kensington Society and Langham Place came many of the chief campaigners for women's issues, including Millicent Fawcett, Elizabeth Garrett Anderson and Barbara Bodichon. These women were more than ready to take on the issue of enfranchisement and the suffrage campaign began in earnest.

In 1865, John Stuart Mill MP included the issue of women's suffrage in his election address. The Kensington Society asked him to present a petition to Parliament and, as one of the arguments against women's suffrage was that women did not want the vote, Mill agreed to present the petition if 100 signatures could be collected. The Society rose to the challenge and within two weeks had collected over 1,500 signatures from all over the United Kingdom, including four from Devon (Catherine, Mary and Ada Johnson from Honiton and May Cockrem from Torquay).[1] When he presented it, Mill argued that it had been organised and signed exclusively by women and therefore clearly demonstrated their desire for the vote. In 1867 he moved an amendment to the Representation of the People Bill to include women. Two Devon MPs, including Walter Morrison, voted for the amendment but it was defeated and the 1867 Representation of the People Act increased the number of men eligible to vote but again excluded women.

On the Campaign Trail

In 1870 a Women's Disabilities (Removal) Bill came before Parliament, drafted by Richard Pankhurst (husband of Emmeline Pankhurst) and introduced by Jacob Bright MP. It proposed that:

> Whenever words import the masculine gender, the same shall be held to include females for all purposes

1832	Representation of the People Act (Reform Act)
1866	John Stuart Mill presents a petition to parliament on women's suffrage
1867	Representation of the People Act (2nd Reform Act)
1870-78	Women's Disabilities (Removal) Bills are brought before parliament
1884	Representation of the People Act (3rd Reform Act)
1897	National Union of Women's Suffrage Societies (NUWSS) is formed
1903	Women's Social and Political Union (WSPU) is formed
1908	Local Branch of the WSPU forms in Plymouth The Anti-Suffrage League is formed with a branch in Plymouth
1909	The Three Towns and District branch of the NUWSS is formed Marion Wallace Dunlop goes on hunger strike Force Feeding introduced
1910	Black Friday (18 November) – WSPU members beaten outside Parliament
1911	Suffrage societies call for women to boycott the census
1913	Emily Wilding Davison is fatally injured at the Epsom Derby NUWSS organises a pilgrimage to London Prisoners Temporary Discharge for Ill Health Act (The Cat and Mouse Act) Mrs Pankhurst arrested at Plymouth
1914	Suffrage activities cease with the outbreak of the First World War
1916	Speakers Conference considers women's suffrage
1918	Representation of the People Act (4th Reform Act)
1928	Representation of the People (Equal Franchise) Act

Fig. 11.1: Timeline of Women's Suffrage Campaign

connected with and having reference to the right to be
registered as voters.

Opponents expressed doubt as to whether the great body
of women were in favour of the franchise. The Bill passed
its second reading but was then defeated at the committee
stage. A similar Bill was put before Parliament several times
between 1871 and 1878. In order to rouse support each
time, meetings were held throughout the country, including
the Three Towns. Millicent Fawcett toured the southwest
in 1871 and on 14 March addressed a public meeting at the
Mechanics' Institute in Plymouth, chaired by William Collier
and reported by the *WMN*. Fawcett had discussed the many,
often contradictory, reasons why women were told they
should not have the vote:

- they were too numerous and if enfranchised would have
  things all their own way,
- they already had things all their own way,
- they were 'angels' unfitted for the political world and
  their exclusion was a privilege,
- women were too easily influenced and handing them the
  vote would be like handing two votes to their men,
- women were so obstinate that there would be endless
  discord in the home.

Fawcett stated that women did not ask for special privileges,
only that where they fulfilled the same conditions as men they
should have the same rights. Against the argument that giving
women the vote would take them away from their domestic
duties she asked 'does any current male voter spend more than
half an hour a week attending to his political duties?' The
speech was well received and it was agreed that a petition would
be presented to Parliament. In April 1871 Walter Morrison
wrote to Millicent Fawcett explaining that he had presented
Gladstone with a memorial signed by 2,400 women.

During an 1872 debate over the Women's Disabilities Bill,
Mr Baillie Cochrane, Conservative MP for Devonport, declared
his opposition to women's suffrage, believing it to be a step

WOMAN'S SUFFRAGE

A PUBLIC MEETING

Will be held at the

MECHANICS' INSTITUTE, ON TUESDAY EVENING

THE 14TH MARCH, AT 8 P.M., WHEN

MRS. FAWCETT

Will Deliver an ADDRESS in favour of Woman's Suffrage.

Mr. W. C. CODLLER will be invited to take the Chair.

Women's Suffrage Meeting with Millicent Fawcett, 9 March 1871. (Western Morning News)

towards a much larger measure. He suggested that if women were admitted to the medical and legal professions then 'it would be necessary to pass an act for the abolition of flirting!'[2] There was, however, significant male support for women's suffrage in the Three Towns. In 1873 the all-male Plymouth City Council passed a resolution in favour of women's suffrage to be passed to the House of Commons.

In 1874 two determined suffragists were on the campaign trail; Miss Caroline Biggs and the American, Miss Beedy who addressed a meeting at the Guildhall, Devonport on 14 December. She explained that women with a legal property qualification should be able to exercise their right to elect Members of Parliament in the same way as they had been doing for councils, school boards and Boards of Guardians. The franchise would be a means to secure better social conditions for women on matters which men tended to legislate according to their own interests, for example the law regarding the guardianship of children. The Mayor thanked Miss Beedy and a resolution was put forward that:

> The exclusion of women otherwise legally qualified for voting for Members of Parliament is injurious to those excluded from the right and is opposed to the principles of just representation and to the law now in force.

Mr Collier seconded the resolution and said for many years he argued against the view that women were too emotional to have the vote. He said emotion was absolutely needed in Parliament, for example in laws protecting children and preventing cruelty to animals.

Despite the failure of further Bills in 1877 and 1878, campaigning continued in the Three Towns. On 17 October 1881 the Bragg sisters held a meeting at their home, Weston Lodge in Mannamead, and the Borough Arms Coffee Tavern was another popular venue. On 16 March 1882, Helen Blackburn, a leading suffragist from Bristol gave a lecture there to the Working Men's Liberal Association on 'The Rise and Progress of the Women's Suffrage Movement'.

In 1883 there was a small majority in favour of the Women's Disabilities (Removal) Bill and the promise of further electoral reform. But despite campaigning from the various suffrage societies, the 1884 Representation of the People Act gave the vote to an extra 6 million working men and once again excluded all women.

On 8 January 1890, Francis Latimer chaired a meeting of the Plymouth Women's Liberal Association and spoke on: 'The position and influence of women in politics'. In the same year a Declaration was published with the names of women householders who would qualify for the vote should they have it. The declaration included three women from the Three Towns – Miss L and Miss E Deeley of 4 Argyle Terrace, and Miss M Bragg of Weston Lodge, Mannamead.[3]

Not all women were convinced however. The *WDM* of 31 May 1889 contained an article, 'A counterblast against woman's suffrage', which described how a formidable reaction against female suffrage had arisen in the ranks of the women themselves. An appeal had been signed by a large number of Plymouth women which stated that:

> While desiring the development of the powers, education and energies of women, they believe that their work for and responsibilities to the state must always

differ essentially from those of men. The opportunities already afforded to women as voters or members of School Boards, Boards of Guardians and other public bodies are regarded with satisfaction by the signatories who however protest against their admission to direct power in the state.

They were concerned that women's quickness of temper would make them 'hotter partisans' than men; that enfranchising married women would be detrimental to family life and that large numbers of women who led immoral lives would have the vote.

By the 1890s there were numerous suffrage groups working across the country. Some groups sought the franchise for all and opposed the exclusion of married women in the suffrage claim, whereas other more conservative suffragists wanted to restrict the franchise to single or widowed women who could claim the same qualifications as men. However, with changes to the laws regarding married women and property in 1893, and the passing of the Local Government Act in 1894 which allowed married women to become eligible for the local government franchise, the 'married women problem' was removed. This paved the way for the unification of suffrage societies and in 1897 the National Union of Women's Suffrage Societies (NUWSS) was formed, with Millicent Fawcett as president.

Suffragists, Suffragettes and the Anti-Suffrage League

At the turn of the century the suffrage movement quietened a little in wake of the Boer War and with the election of a Conservative government. However in 1903, with the prospect of another Liberal government, suffrage voices were again raised, and this time with a more radical tone.

Frustrated that forty years of polite petitioning and campaigning had achieved nothing, Emmeline Pankhurst founded the Women's Social and Political Union (WSPU).

They had one purpose – political equality with men – and they advocated direct action under the slogan 'Deeds Not Words'. They claimed that men had employed aggression to win their own franchise, although some argued that such aggression had been a side-effect of protest, whereas the WSPU planned militant action from the outset. Nevertheless the group attracted members and they began a campaign of demonstrations and disruption of political meetings. The Daily Mail termed them 'suffragettes', and though meant as a derogatory term, the WSPU adopted it with relish. Suffragettes wore green, white and purple to distinguish themselves from the green, white and red of the NUWSS.

On 8 April 1908, Miss Annie Kenney, the West of England organiser for the WSPU addressed a meeting at the Athenaeum, Plymouth on 'Why women need the vote'. She said that women did not want the vote because they wanted to be like men but rather that a woman's point of view was just as worthy of consideration. It was announced that a local branch of the WSPU was to be formed, and the *WMN* of 16 May 1908 advertised a meeting of the Three Towns & District WSPU at the Corn Exchange with Annie Kenney as speaker.

Miss Kenney was tireless. On 20 May she addressed a crowded meeting at Stoke Public Hall, Devonport and on 21 May she spoke outside the dockyard gates in Catherine Street, Devonport. Apparently listened to with interest by a large number of dockyard workers, Miss Kenney spoke of how women were tired of being told that they must 'wait just a little longer' by the government. There was also an announcement that the local branch were organising an excursion to Hyde Park for the rally planned for 21 June; over 200 women were expected to attend from the Three Towns. The rally became known as 'Women's Sunday' and was the first large-scale meeting organised by the WSPU.

The newspapers printed letters from those who disagreed with the activities of the suffragettes. On 4 September 1908 'Beatrice D' wrote to say that: 'nine-tenths of what they write and speak is damaging to their cause'. She took particular offence at the pity shown by the suffragettes for a woman imprisoned for stealing bread for her children. Beatrice thought that prison would be a welcome break for such a woman and a respite from the 'one room home, drunken husband and four children who would be better off in the workhouse'. She compared listening to Miss Kenney as listening to 'the ravings of a delirious person'. A reply of 7 September took umbrage at Beatrice D and replied to her question of 'what good purpose do the suffragettes serve?' with:

> For forty years there have been women's suffrage societies doing their best to get votes for women but this has proved inadequate. Until the WSPU started their agitation few were aware of these societies but now it is the name of Pankhurst which springs readily to mind … the present tactics have raised the question of votes for women from an academic dream to a question of practical politics … every statement Miss Kenney uttered could be proved to the hilt.

It is thought that the WSPU opened a shop in Plymouth but the record of its location has not survived. WSPU correspondence

Meetings, &c.

THREE TOWNS AND DISTRICT WOMEN'S
SOCIAL AND POLITICAL UNION.

VOTES FOR WOMEN
A MASS MEETING FOR WOMEN ONLY,

MONDAY, MAY 18th, CORN EXCHANGE, PLYMOUTH,
AT 7.30 P.M.
Speaker ...... Miss ANNIE KENNEY,
(National W.S.P.U.)
ADMISSION FREE.   COLLECTION.

Meeting of the Three Towns and District WSPU, 16 May 1908. (Western Morning News)

was addressed to 11 Albert Street, the Hoe, so this could be a possible location and a drawing-room meeting was held there in November 1908 with Miss Morden and Miss Elsie Howey in attendance.

In November 1908 the WSPU had plans to make their presence known during Prime Minister Herbert Asquith's visit to Devonport on 7 November for the launch of the battleship HMS *Collingwood*. The *WMN* reported afterwards that the demonstration had been a quiet affair, but that Asquith was heavily protected by police and the visit carefully controlled with ticket only access to the platform at North Road station. When a cry of 'here's a suffragette!' went up near the corner of Tavistock Street, the 'slim, girlish figure' wearing green, white and purple and a Votes for Women badge was closely monitored by the police. She walked the crowds quietly distributing handbills which advertised a forthcoming meeting to be addressed by Mrs Pethick-Lawrence. In the same paper the suffragettes stated that they had managed to throw bills and literature into Asquith's carriage but that several felt he had been let off too lightly. A letter on official Three Towns WSPU stationery had been posted to reach Asquith at dinner that evening. It said:

> The above union would like to ask Mr Asquith why the Liberal Government does not live up to its alleged principle in relation to the demand for votes for women.

On 30 November the *WMN* reported that a contingent of local suffragettes assembled on Mutley railway station to bid farewell to Mrs Pethick-Lawrence who had been speaking in the Three Towns and she departed to cries of 'Votes for Women!'

Opposition to women's suffrage continued. In 1906 William Cremer, in a speech to the House of Commons, argued that 'women are creatures of impulse and emotion and did not decide questions on the grounds of reason as men did'. In 1908 he approached the author Mary Humphrey Ward and asked her to become president of the Anti-Suffrage League (ASL) and on 8 July 1908 the organisation published its first manifesto. The league was established not just as a protest against the military tactics of the suffragettes but to actively oppose women having the vote and it drew considerable female support.

The *North Devon Gazette* of 17 November 1908 reported on an ASL meeting in Plymouth, addressed by the organising secretary Miss Dickens. It was decided to open a Plymouth branch and Mrs Spender, the Mayoress, was elected president. The League agreed that, while women should have the local or municipal vote, they should not receive the parliamentary vote as it would weaken the power of the state and give women an inappropriate voice in matters such as the military, which were not their proper concern. Their interests would continue to be served by their male companions. Petitions against women's suffrage were extensively signed and the ASL produced a series of postcards which ridiculed suffragettes, depicting them as either husbandless harridans, or wives and mothers neglecting their families. *The Western Times* of 14 August 1909 reported that the League numbered 9,000 members across the country.

With the WSPU and the ASL established, the NUWSS also formed a Three Towns branch. Drawing room meetings had been held early in 1909 and in a letter to the *WMN* of 13 May 1909, Dr Mabel Ramsay confirmed the formal inauguration of the Three Towns and District Branch. The sole object of the society was to obtain the parliamentary vote on the same terms 'as it was or might be granted to men'. Their methods would be orderly propaganda and public discussion and they would be for women who wanted the vote but without militant tactics. Their first annual meeting was held at the Corn Exchange on 4 April 1910.

The 1911 census collection was to include more searching questions on family life, such as length of marriage and the number of children, both living and dead in an attempt to collect data which could be used for welfare reform and to curb infant mortality. However, many women saw it as an intrusion into their most intimate lives from a government which steadfastly denied them the right to vote and there was a call to boycott the census. Both the WSPU and NUWSS supported the boycott under the banner of 'women do not count, neither shall we be counted'. Dr Ramsay held a census resistance party at her home in Plymouth. Upwards of twenty women slept on couches and floors and refused to fill in the details of the census form. The census page at the National Archives shows that Dr Ramsay, her mother and a boarder had filled in only their names, three servants were listed as 'names unknown' and across the page in large letters has been written simply 'Suffragettes'. When census records for 1911 were released, researchers hoped to determine just how widespread the census boycott had been. Surprisingly they found that several quite prominent suffragettes and suffragists had signed the census. Much had been made in the press of the proposed boycott hindering welfare reform and as many suffrage supporters had improvements to women's and children's lives at the heart of their personal campaign this may have been a hard pill to swallow. A prominent WSPU member in Stockport complied with the census when it might have been expected that she would resist. But the details she provided show that of the five children she bore, two had died.[4]

The Conciliation Bill and an Increase in Militancy

In 1910 matters were looking brighter for the cause. A Conciliation Committee had been formed, composed of cross-party MPs all in favour of some form of women's enfranchisement. They drafted a Bill which they hoped would have the support of all but the most ardent anti-suffragist. The WSPU had agreed a truce while the Bill was debated and the NUWSS acknowledged that, while the Bill was more restrictive than they had hoped, they could not deny its importance. After a two-day debate the Bill was carried by a majority of 109 votes and sent to be amended by a House of Commons committee. All looked promising for its passing – until Asquith dissolved his government and called for a general election before the task could be completed, effectively vetoing the Bill.

The response of the WSPU was immediate. Three hundred women descended on the House of Commons on Friday

THE VOTE.
WHEN THEY GET IT.

Anti-Suffrage League Postcard. (Authors Own)

18 November, to demand an audience with the prime minister. The police responded with unprecedented brutality and for over six hours the women were beaten and thrown against walls, railings and pavements. *The Mirror* published a photograph of a suffragette lying on the ground with her hands over her face surrounded by men and the day became known as Black Friday.

A second Conciliation Bill was drafted and passed on 5 May 1911 but there was much opposition to it from the new Parliament. Winston Churchill objected as he saw it as undemocratic, denying votes to honest, working-class wives. David Lloyd George opposed it as he saw it as just handing more votes to the Conservatives. Asquith then announced that he would be introducing a Bill to enfranchise the 4 million men currently excluded from the vote and suggested that this could be amended to include women. Millicent Fawcett retained her faith in the government but the WSPU were suspicious, believing that this new Bill, which would effectively give the vote to 7 million women, would actually mean no vote at all as it would be impossible for the government to pass such controversial legislation. The second Conciliation Bill was debated in March 1912 and defeated by fourteen votes. Asquith claimed that his party did not back it because they were committed to his proposed Full Franchise Bill – but this Bill never appeared before parliament. This betrayal by the Liberal government galvanised both the NUWSS and the WSPU to greater measures. Millicent Fawcett who had previously urged the NUWSS to work with any party candidate who supported women's suffrage now lost all confidence in the Liberal Party, believing that the only route to success lay with a change of government. The NUWSS was directed to work to this end and took the decision to form an alliance with the growing Labour party, although this was to the discomfort of some of their members. The WSPU, which had already taken the stance of opposing Liberal candidates at elections to 'punish the government' and try to force a change in its policies, simply upped their militancy.

They began to favour campaigns such as smashing windows and firing empty houses rather than their earlier large scale public demonstrations. Those arrested for such action only brought publicity to the campaign, particularly due to the hunger strike – the suffragette protest of choice since Marion Wallace Dunlop began the action in July 1909. *The Western Times* of 21 April 1914 claimed that the incendiary campaign of 1913 had caused losses amounting to a quarter of a million pounds.

In April 1913 Winston Churchill visited Plymouth as 1st Lord of the Admiralty. Suffragettes daubed Smeaton's Tower with white paint, writing on the Sound side: 'To Churchill. No security till you give women votes, no matter how big the navy' and on the city side: 'To save the State from shipwreck, give women the vote'. Shelters were also graffitied – one read: 'To Churchill. No rest for government while they torture us women', and another simply: 'Votes for Women'. Suffragettes were also blamed for cutting telephone wires at Lipson and there was an apparent attempt to blow up Smeaton's Tower with a bomb. A can filled with black powder was found at the foot of the tower, but although a paraffin-soaked wick had been lit it had not properly ignited.[5]

The NUWSS took a different stance, concerned that such behaviour would just prove that women were unfit for political life. A peaceful pilgrimage to London was organised in 1913 with women marching along eight different routes to convene at Hyde Park on 26 July for a huge open air meeting. This was partly to contrast with the militant tactics of the WSPU, but also to prove how many women supported the campaign. The southwest 'pilgrims' left Lands End on 19 June and arrived in Plymouth ten days later. Wearing their white, red and green sashes they were met by a group of supporters from Devonport and given a police escort through Plymouth. They lunched at Dr Ramsay's house, held an open air meeting in Victoria Park and an evening meeting at the Corn Exchange. A further meeting at Plympton saw them pelted with rotten eggs and tomatoes. Twenty-five women then joined the march to London, including Dr Ramsay's mother, who became known as 'The old lady from Land's End'. The group joined around 50,000 women at Hyde Park and delivered the message: 'The women of the west demand votes for women'.

In 1913 the Prisoners Temporary Discharge for Health Act was introduced – the Cat and Mouse Act – in an attempt to control the chaos caused by hunger strikes and the brutal practice of force-feeding. Women were held down and a tube inserted into the stomach either nasally or orally. If the tube was to be passed down the throat, the jaw was forced open by a wooden or steel gag which was twisted behind the back teeth. Liquid was then poured down the tube, but many women simply vomited it straight back up and the process began over again. The practice was highly controversial and threatened to increase support for the suffragettes. The Cat and Mouse Act allowed for a hunger-striking prisoner, certified in danger of death by prison doctors, to be released until she regained her health. She would then be re-arrested to finish her sentence.

In October 1913, Emmeline Pankhurst was out of prison under the Cat and Mouse Act. She travelled to the USA for a lecture and fundraising tour and sailed for England in November with her ship due to dock at Plymouth. It was expected that she would be arrested on landing and newspaper reports describe 5,000 women descending on the town, distributing themselves around quays, railway stations and docks ready to intercept Mrs Pankhurst if possible. A huge crowd gathered at the Great Western Docks including members of the press and a group of women called 'Mrs Pankhurst's bodyguard', under the leadership of Gertrude Harding. Mrs Dacre Fox wrote in the *Burnley News* of 13 December 1913 that the bodyguard had the express purpose of preventing Mrs Pankhurst's arrest. They carried wooden 'Indian' clubs commonly used in exercise and had been trained in the art of jiu-jitsu by Edith Garrud, a member of the WSPU. Jiu-jitsu employed minimal violence, using an opponent's strength and weight against them, and was a socially acceptable activity for women. The *Western Times* of 5 December 1913 reported on the circumstances of Mrs Pankhurst's arrest. The Chief Constable of Plymouth had received instructions days before the liner was due to dock and, wanting to avoid scenes of riot, he arranged for the liner to anchor in the outer harbour. He went out on a police tender accompanied by officers from Scotland Yard and Plymouth and a prison wardress. The local press were conveyed on a tender, hoping to reach the liner and interview Mrs Pankhurst, but they were stopped about two miles out until the police had completed their arrest. Mrs Pankhurst had been sent a telegram from WSPU headquarters informing her that she would be arrested on arrival. In her book *My Own Story* she recounts how the liner came to anchor in the outer harbour and the bay, normally teeming with vessels, was clear of all craft. The tender which would normally meet the liner was anchored between two warships which served to screen the view from the shore. A fisherman's dory dashed across the harbour and two women stood up in the boat as it passed the liner shouting 'The cats are here, Mrs Pankhurst....'

Once the Chief Constable was on board, Mrs Pankhurst was arrested. She asked that she could be accompanied ashore and it was agreed that Mrs Childe Dorr would stay with her. Prior to the arrival of the police, the money raised on the tour of the USA, some £4,500, had been sewn into the garments of Mrs Childe Dorr to prevent the authorities from seizing it.

TO THE MEN AND WOMEN IN THIS THEATRE !

DO YOU REALISE THAT

Mrs. PANKHURST

Has been arrested again to-day on her arrival from America ?

ARE YOU GOING TO LET HER SUFFER IN PRISON while Sir Edward Carson & Mr. Bonar Law are allowed to go free.

Think it over and then DEMAND HER INSTANT RELEASE !

Printed by G. Oliver & Co., Ltd., 73-75, Lower Thames St., E.C.

Notice distributed to unnamed theatre after Mrs Pankhurst's arrest in Plymouth. (Mary Evans Picture Library)

The police tender then docked at Bull Point, a government landing stage closed to the public. There was much speculation in the newspapers immediately following the arrest as to where Mrs Pankhurst would be taken. The *Western Times* of 5 December made much of the 'outwitting of the suffragettes', describing them as 'the Shrieking Sisterhood', patrolling Plymouth and Devonport, being 'led a wild goosechase by local wags', and promising violence to the 'valuable property and plate-glass windows of Plymouth'. Mrs Pankhurst was actually taken across Dartmoor to Exeter Prison where she immediately went on hunger strike. Afterwards she described the governor and wardresses as kind and openly sympathetic. She was released after four days in a state of near collapse, and taken to the Great Western Hotel. From there she travelled to London, being told to return to prison after a week. Instead she travelled to Paris.

The *Western Times* of 16 December 1913 reported that after the arrest in Plymouth, a huge fire broke out at a timber yard in Richmond Walk, Devonport. An acre and a half of timber plus a part of Hancock's Pleasure Fair, including a scenic railway, were

The Southwest Pilgrims on the 1913 March to London. (Mary Evans Picture Library)

The Southwest Pilgrims Meet in Exeter on the way to London 1913. (Mary Evans Picture Library)

destroyed. The cause of the fire was never officially determined but it was claimed it was in retaliation for the arrest. A copy of *The Suffragette* was found at the scene and two postcards which read: 'Our reply to the torture of Mrs Pankhurst and her cowardly arrest here,' and, 'To the Government. How dare you arrest Mrs Pankhurst and allow Sir Edward Carson and Mr Bonar Law to go free?' Notices were also distributed in a local, unnamed theatre.

Suffrage and the First World War

Two days after Britain declared war on Germany both the NUWSS and the WSPU announced a suspension of all political activity and in return for the release of all suffrage prisoners the WSPU agreed to end militant activities and help the war effort. By 1916 however, the question of universal suffrage was being discussed again in parliament.

Before 1914, forty per cent of men were still disenfranchised as they did not meet property qualifications and MPs were keen to allow men in military service and those working in other military-useful industries to vote. Women's suffrage was also being considered, given the contribution that women were making to the war effort. A cross-party, cross-house body was set up to consider the matter and make recommendations to the House of Commons, chaired (apparently reluctantly) by the Speaker of the House who endeavoured to have a balance of opinions on the committee. Millicent Fawcett and other suffrage campaigners lobbied committee members and the issue of women's suffrage again began to appear in the newspapers.

The *Western Times* of 13 October 1916 reported on a meeting addressed by Mrs Fawcett. She spoke of the upcoming Speaker's Conference and that though the prospects for women were good, they must not be satisfied with a solution on the basis of the old Conciliation Bill as this would not touch women who most needed the franchise – those working in the factories. It was also remarked that women were being taunted with only doing their duty during the war in order to get the vote and that this was most unfair.

In a letter to the editor in the *WMN* of 18 November 1916, a number of signatories confirmed that their opposition to women's suffrage had not changed because of the war. They saw only two options – to refuse all women the vote or to sanction universal suffrage which would give females an unacceptable majority of nearly one-and-a-half million votes. The term 'petticoat government' was used to stress the influence that women might have. The old issue of women not wanting the vote was again raised. Mrs A Ramsay, Dr Ramsay's mother, replied to say that she was horrified that there were still those who would withhold the vote from women. To those who claimed that women do not want the vote, she replied that it would be entirely voluntary and that women did not want the vote as a 'reward'.

The debate on women's suffrage was left to the end of the Speaker's Conference. In early January 1917 the conference agreed to consider the issue by eighteen votes to four. The proposal that there should be some measure of women's suffrage was passed by fifteen votes to six, but a motion that this should be on the same terms as men was lost twelve votes to ten. It was then proposed that the vote should go to occupiers, or wives of occupiers, and this was passed nine to eight – so by a majority of one the women's suffrage clause went forward. There was still opposition but the Bill was put forward to both houses and on 28 March 1917, Parliament passed the Women's Suffrage Bill by 341 votes to 62. Finally, in February 1918, The Representation of the People Act gave the vote to all men aged 21 and over (and to men aged 19 and over on military and naval service) and to women aged 30 or older who were householders, wives of householders, occupiers of a property with an annual rent of £5, or graduates of British universities, enfranchising around 8 million women. The reasoning behind the age limit was that women matured later than men and those younger than 30 would not have the same ability to reason. Suffrage societies were surprised by the majority that voted in favour of the bill, given that previous attempts had been so vehemently opposed.

It has been suggested that the eventual franchise was a 'reward' for women's war work rather than due to pressure by suffrage campaigners, but this has recently been questioned. There is no doubt that the militancy of the suffragettes shocked and angered many, but it also ensured that women's suffrage was kept in the public eye. If the decision had been made to enfranchise all men over 21 but to still deny any woman the vote, this would no doubt have vastly swelled the ranks of the suffragettes after the war.

The Campaign for Equal Franchise

Although the 1918 Act was a victory of sorts, it still failed to enfranchise a huge number of women and, ironically, excluded

Smeaton's Tower. (Chris Glasspool)

many of the young women who had campaigned so tirelessly. The fight for equal suffrage continued.

The WSPU was disbanded and Emmeline Pankhurst went on to form a Women's Party. The NUWSS continued to press for full equality with men but when Millicent Fawcett resigned from political life in 1919 and was succeeded by Eleanor Rathbone, the NUWSS was replaced by a new organisation, the National Union of Societies for Equal Citizenship (NUSEC) which adopted a six-point plan:

- Equal pay for equal work and an open field for women in industry and the professions,
- Equal standard of sex morals between men and women with reform of divorce laws and all laws dealing with solicitation and prostitution,
- Legislation to provide pensions for civilian widows with dependent children,
- Equalisation of the franchise,
- Legal recognition of mothers as equal guardians with fathers of their children,
- Opening of the legal profession and the magistracy to women.

The Plymouth Citizens' Association took the place of the NUWSS and was affiliated to NUSEC. It was open to both men and women with the aim of educating women voters and keeping a view on matters affecting the local community. On 28 May 1919 in the conference hall Plymouth, the last annual meeting of the Plymouth NUWSS was held, and on 2 June 1919 the Plymouth Citizens' Association was inaugurated.

On 24 February 1921, the *WMN* reported that Dr Ramsay held an 'at-home' for members of the PCA. Miss Tann of NUSEC spoke, and apart from the matter of equal franchise, other matters were discussed such as pensions for widows with dependent children. Mrs Daymond, presiding, said that they must induce more women to stand at the next Plymouth Council elections and to include more women on council committees, particularly as a new committee was soon to be established dealing with maternity and child welfare.

The PCA continued to meet regularly. On 29 June 1922 the *WMN* reported that Lady Astor and other MPs were to ask the prime minister to receive a deputation organised by NUSEC to present memorials signed by 200 MPs and over 200 organisations asking for the equal franchise. But on 17 July 1922 when David Lloyd George was asked whether the government intended, either during the present session or during the lifetime of the present parliament, to pass a bill granting the equal franchise to women, his answer was no.

On 4 May 1923 a Conference of Women was held at Plymouth, the first of its kind held in the southwest. On the agenda was the demand for equal citizenship for women, the right of married women to work on equal terms with single women, and the issue of women police officers in all towns and cities. Miss Beaumont of NUSEC spoke and said the object of the association was to obtain all such reforms necessary to secure real equality of liberty, status and opportunity between men and women. They were indebted to Plymouth-born Mr Isaac Foot MP, for introducing an Equal Franchise Bill, although it was understood that this was more in the way of a demonstration and they did not expect it to be carried.

Bills for equal franchise were put to the House of Commons throughout the early to mid-1920s with no success. The same old anti-suffrage arguments were raised again and again; that the majority of women did not want the vote; that women under 30 were too 'incompetent' for politics; that women's votes would outnumber men's.

In July 1926 women marched from the Embankment to Hyde Park in a nod to the marches and processions of the old suffrage campaigns. On 26 November 1926 the *WMN* reported that Miss Helen Ward for NUSEC had spoken to the Plymouth Citizens' Association stating that only one in fifteen women in industry was as yet enfranchised. The government had given a pledge that all women should have the vote but this had been put off time and again.

Finally, on 2 July 1928, royal assent was given to The Representation of the People (Equal Franchise) Act which gave the parliamentary vote to all women on the same basis as men. Fittingly, Dame Millicent Fawcett was in attendance at the House of Commons for the event, as she was when John Stuart Mill moved the first women's suffrage amendment to the Representation of the People Bill in 1867. Dame Fawcett had seen the women's suffrage movement through from start to finish over a period of sixty-one years. Emmeline Pankhurst had died only a few weeks earlier, on 14 June 1928.

CHAPTER 12

Jobs for the Girls

'The capable and efficient woman can undertake practically every occupation...'

Census records provide a great deal of information about how women were employed over the decades. Figure 12.2 shows the number of women employed in various occupations in Plymouth and Devonport, taken from the 1841 census. Only sixteen per cent of women were in occupations, compared to fifty-seven per cent of men, and of the total workforce, twenty-seven per cent were women. Eighty-three per cent of the female workforce was employed in the domestic service, textile and laundry trades. Of some of the more unusual occupations for the time there were a handful of carpenters, clockmakers, gardeners and one mineralogist – the only one in the whole of Devon.

Women and the Dockyard

Devonport dockyard was the major employer for the Three Towns, underpinning its economy and shaping the lives of its population. Although employment for women within the dockyard was limited, during the early nineteenth century, opportunities did arise in the specific areas of rope- and colour- (flag) making.

In 1805, a handful of women were employed as colour-makers, paid the same rate as men of 20*d* per day.[1] Women were also employed as twine-spinners in the first stage of rope-making. Newspapers reported on the presentation of gifts and pensions to twine-spinners for long service. On 28 September 1863 the

1844	Factory Act: children to work a maximum 9 hour day, women and young workers a maximum 12 hour day
1847	Factory Act: limits women and children to a 10 hour day in textile mills. Subsequent Acts extend this to other factories
1878	Factory Act: limits women workers to a 56 hour week. Minimum age for employment is ten
1891	Factory Act: minimum age raised to eleven. Women not to be employed or re-employed within four weeks of childbirth
1919	Sex Disqualification (Removals) Act: women no longer barred from civil or judicial office or the professions
1944	Marriage bar removed from teaching and the BBC
1946	Marriage bar removed from the civil service (except Foreign Office)
1970	Equal Pay Act: men and women have right to equal pay for equal work or work of equal value
1973	Marriage bar removed from the Foreign Office
1975	Sex Discrimination Act: protects men and women from discrimination on the grounds of sex or marital status

Employment Protection Act: introduces the first maternity leave legislation |
| **1993** | Employment Rights Act: maternity leave extended to all women workers |
| **2010** | Equality Act replaces all other legislation |

Fig. 12.1: Timeline of Employment Legislation

Devonport + Plymouth 1841	Males	Females
Total Population	**35056**	**45003**
Of Independent Means	912	3461
Pensioner/Paupers etc	1035	490
Others (prisoners, miners, lunatics)	515	34
No occupation (includes children)	13372	33660
Total in Occupations	**19222**	**7358**

Number of Women Employed in Various Occupations	
Domestic Servant	3968
Textile Trades: Dressmaker/Milliner etc	1550
Laundry Keeper/Washerwoman	285
Grocer/Tea Dealer	199
Charwoman	193
Teacher	166
Boot/Shoe Maker	159
Nurse/Midwife	158
Shopkeeper	58
Lodging House Keeper	52
Publican/Beer Shop	48
Greengrocer	39
Fishmonger	24
Labourer	18
Head/Keeper Public Institution	17
Rope/Cord Spinner	16
Fisherwoman	12
Cabinet maker/Upholsterer	10
Milk Seller/Cow Keeper	10
Butcher	9
Poulterer	8
Jeweller	6
Bookseller/Binder/Publisher	5

Fig. 12.2: Female Occupations in Plymouth and Devonport, 1841

WDM recorded the superannuation of Miss Hocking and the presentation of a family bible by other twine-spinners as a mark of respect for her twenty-six years of service. By the mid-nineteenth century parts of the rope-making process, including twine-spinning, had become mechanised. In January 1867, the *WDM* reported that a large number of male rope-makers were to be discharged and either given early superannuation or kept on as general labourers. However, employment on the rope-house machines would be offered to women and the positions seem to have been reserved for widows and dependants of deceased dockyard workers. Devonport Naval Heritage Centre has several letters from petitioners requesting that widows and daughters be considered for the work. The following is a transcript of a letter dated 27 April 1868 from Mary Western to the Admiral Superintendent:

> The petition of Mary Western humbly and respectfully … that your petitioner is the widow of John Western who had served in the capacity of cook in Her Majesty's Navy for a period of eight years he having died about six years since leaving three children wholly dependent on your petitioner for support one of whom is a girl Elizabeth Maria aged 18 years who is very desirous of being entered in Her Majesty's ropery as machinist.
>
> Under these circumstances your petitioner humbly … your honour will give the case your favourable consideration and your petitioner, duty bound will ever pray.
> Mary Western

The letter was accompanied by another from a church minister in support of the petition:

> I with great confidence, having known Mary Western and her daughter Elizabeth Maria for a period of six years, beg to state that they are both very deserving of any patronage your honour can bestow on the daughter….

> They are hardworking and industrious doing their very
> best for an honest living.

There are several other letters in the archives including two on behalf of Mrs Wilsmore, widow of George Wilsmore, a former sick berth steward who died on board ship. He had made no provision for his wife and six children and the letters ask for her to be considered as a spinner. The application appears to have been successful because the 1871 census shows Jemima Wilsmore employed as a machinist at the dockyard along with her son Thomas, age 14, who was employed as a rope-house boy.

Women may have been targeted for these new mechanised roles because they were a flexible and cheap workforce, whereas unionised male workers often opposed such changes.[2] At the dockyard in Chatham the Master Attendant commented that women were more attentive, steady, and more contented with their pay.[3] The last point is particularly telling. The dockyards were run at enormous cost and the Admiralty were constantly looking to reduce expenditure. The women were poorly paid and there is evidence that they applied for poor relief despite being employed full-time.[4] In 1875 a raft of petitions were submitted by the women regarding the intention to reduce their dinner time from seventy-five to thirty minutes. The longer lunch had given the women, many of them widows with children, time to prepare food for their families, but the new hours prevented this. Whilst the Admiral Superintendent of Devonport was sympathetic and asked for an exception, this was denied.[5]

On 19 April 1875 the *WMN* described the work in the ropery:

> The small regiment of women are in attendance to feed
> the machines, ensure their smooth-running and to mend
> broken thread. They work in a well-lit loft full of whirling
> machinery and in an atmosphere charged with 'fluff'

from which they protect themselves by wearing quaint caps and gowns of coarse hessian. Men bring the hemp to the loft but all the operations within are conducted solely by women, 128 of them in all. Each woman can produce six times the amount by machine per day than could be produced by hand and as they are paid by piece work they get as much from the machines as possible. They have a comfortable dining-hall adjoining the loft with an oven for cooking and are under the direction of a matron.

This gives a fairly pleasant view of the spinning-loft, but the 'fluff' which charged the atmosphere would have been constantly breathed in. There was also the risk of industrial accidents and in the 1869 Report on the Health of the Navy, the Devonport Staff Surgeon records an accident where an 18-year-old machine-girl caught her right hand in the spinning machinery. Although she was treated she caught tetanus and died.[6]

The work was subject to the fluctuations of demand and workers could be laid off or put onto short hours with little notice. In January 1880 there were reports that twenty-two women and boys would be discharged. As it had been usual to allow women three months leave for maternity purposes it was decided that all probable candidates for leave of that description would be discharged first. It is unclear whether this refers to those already pregnant or any woman of child-bearing age.

Census reports from 1901 and 1911 do not record rope-making as an individual occupation so it is difficult to confirm whether the women machinists carried on. The 1921 census however, does list rope-maker as an occupation in Plymouth, employing forty-five women and forty-eight men. By that time women had been heavily employed at the dockyard during the First World War and would be again during the Second.

Restrictions on Women's Employment

Employment reform was one of the major concerns of the emerging feminist movement of the mid-nineteenth century. Campaigners argued that employment restrictions placed on women denied them self-development and perpetuated the view that women were beholden to their men and domestic life for both income and self-worth.

There were many factors which restricted the opportunities women had in the workplace. Increasing industrialisation through the nineteenth century separated home from work and tended to exclude women – census data suggests that female employment was higher in the early nineteenth century than any recorded again until after the Second World War.[7] The ideology of different spheres for men and women had become very powerful by the late nineteenth century and there was much debate over which, if any, employment was suitable for women. Their place was in the home, caring for the family as the 'angel in the house', and employment was generally considered unrespectable. This concept however did not account for the plight of spinsters who could rarely afford to be ladies of leisure, or working-class women who had no option but to work. These women were affected by another concept which arose during the nineteenth century – that of the 'family wage'. Trade unions pressed for a man's wage to be set at a level to support his family. In her 1930s book *Women Workers and the Industrial Revolution*, Ivy Pinchbeck wrote that the family wage was a 'boon' for women, saving them from the double burden of domestic work and employment. However the reality of the family wage was that women's wages were up to fifty per cent lower than men's, even when they were working on the same processes, and women rarely had access to higher-grade, higher paid, occupations. In 1909 the Trade Board for the tailoring industry set an hourly rate of 3¼*d* for women and 6*d* for men.[8] Widows, single women living independently with or without dependants and married women whose husbands were poorly paid or out of work were often placed in dire poverty.

It was also the common view that a woman's childbearing function must always take priority over her employment, particularly in the early twentieth century when poor general health led to concerns over the future of the nation. The legislation of the Factory Acts regulated female labour, restricting the hours that women could work in an increasing number of occupations. By 1891 women workers in factories were restricted to a fifty-six-hour week and employers were prohibited from employing women within four weeks of childbirth. While the aim of these acts was to protect the health of women and children, the effect was to restrict the amount women could earn and added to their struggles.

Working Women in Plymouth

From the mid-nineteenth to early twentieth century, census details show that the bulk of women's work was in trades associated with female skills, especially where these were casual or low paid. Over the country as a whole, domestic service was the single largest employer – the census of 1851 showed that forty per cent of women in provincial cities and fifty per cent in London were so employed – with textiles and the clothing industry a close second. The 1851 census for the Three Towns shows that over seventy-five per cent of employed women were in these trades. Two offices in Plymouth which matched domestic servants with employers were run by Jane Watton of Russell Street and Annie Watton of York Street.[9] But although domestic service was considered a respectable occupation it was hard work with poor pay and conditions. It also tended to favour the young – there were fewer opportunities for married, or older single women, and these women often turned to charring or laundry work. The 1901 census report for Devon showed that of 629 retired domestic servants, 389 were in the workhouse.

Census details for the Three Towns indicate that large numbers of women were not in any occupation throughout the decades but it is difficult to determine how many of these women were in active need of work. Women might not declare their occupation on the census perhaps because it was casual or seasonal, illegal or they wanted to keep the income secret from their husbands. However, other sources suggest that there was a large population of unemployed women in the Three Towns, living in poverty. The *WDM* of 1 March 1862 reported on 'this every-day increasing disability'. One suggestion had been that male shop assistants should make way for girls, but the newspaper reported that 'ladies who went shopping' preferred the attentions of a male attendant:

> There is something that attracts the ladies to a new dress when displayed by an attendant with whiskers … and calico goes off much better when recommended by a masculine smile.

Employers also felt there were some jobs which were too heavy for girls to perform so between the ladies who shopped and the shop owners themselves, women were denied such positions. There was no doubt that there were more women looking for employment than opportunities existed which ultimately led them to the poorhouses, jails and streets.

There were women carving out their own careers. The 1881 census lists Harriett J. Boolds, daughter of a dockyard shipwright, as a draper in Devonport. She employed twenty-eight assistants, eight milliners, five dressmakers, six apprentices and three porters. In 1838, at the age of 22, she opened a small haberdashery shop in Pond Lane, Devonport and with her brother Edwin, grew the business into HJ & EA Boolds, opening other shops in the town. She died in 1896 but the business carried on, closing in the 1920s. The Boolds name was revived when, in 1931, her nephew's wife and daughter opened a draper's shop in Plymouth. It finally closed in 1985.[10]

Another woman in business was Ann Farley, the widow of baker, Samuel Farley. Ann continued the business after his death and is listed in the 1871 census as baker and head of household at 5 Bretonside. Ann was asked by a local surgeon to manufacture an infant cereal biscuit which he had devised – the forerunner of

Farley's Rusks. The recipe for Rusks passed via Ann's son Edwin to William Trahair who continued to employ Ann's granddaughter Miss Morley. Trahair's business was eventually sold to Glaxo Laboratories Ltd and Farley's Rusks were manufactured in Plymouth until 1990.[11] Ann is honoured with a blue plaque near the site of the old Bretonside bakery.

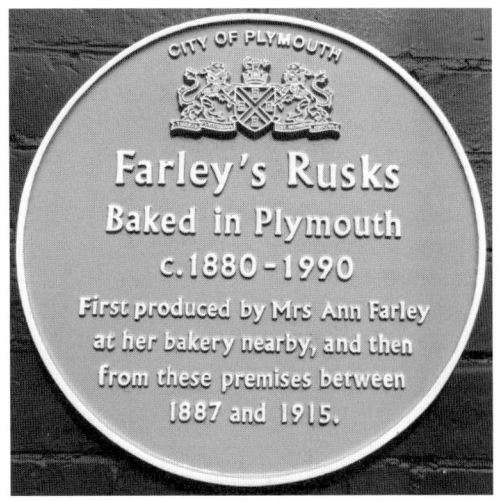

Blue Plaque near site of Anne Farley's Bakery. (Chris Glasspool)

The Changing Jobs Market

As well as census records, the 'Situations Vacant' columns of newspapers give an interesting picture of what employment opportunities there were throughout the decades. Through the 1850s to 1870s, advertisements for women tended to be restricted to domestic servants and the textiles and dressmaking trades. It is also interesting how often the adverts specify men for example in the *WMN* of January 1871:

- *Clerk for Merchant's office – married man required*
- *Experienced young man wanted as waiter*
- *Grocer's assistant – experienced young man*
- *Steady single man wanted for milking/gardening/general jobs around farmhouse*
- *Grainer/writer/marbler – none but steady and competent men need apply.*

But there were gradual changes. On 21 July 1885 the *WMN* advertised for intelligent young men to apply for the civil service. Eight years later a similar advert also invited young ladies to apply.

	Males	Females Unmarried	Females Married
Total Population	**77319**	**32630**	**46135**
Retired	4366	178	194
Living on own Means	246	836	1175
Other (inc students)	8942	15256	39907
Engaged in Occupations	**63765**	**16360**	**4859**
Domestic Service[a]	854	6644	1744
Dressmakers/Tailors/Milliners	1782	3976	863
Professions[b]	1765	1636	339
Lodging/Hospitality[c]	4424	1126	1084
Textiles/Fabrics	508	1123	151
Commercial[e]	2621	581	28
General/Shopkeepers/Undefined	5607	364	430
Printers/Publishers/Stationary	1028	320	52
General/Local Government	2015	133	43
Wood Furniture/Fittings[f]	1120	130	55
Chemicals[e]	598	98	17
Engineering/Metals/Vehicles	9419	53	7
Transport	7199	49	4
Precious Metals[e]	377	42	17
Skins/Leather[e]	144	32	11
Brick/Cement/Pottery/Glass[e]	36	26	3
Agriculture	562	24	4
Mines and Quarries	278	3	5
Defence/Military	17849	0	0
Fishing	427	0	0
Building[d]	4548	0	1
Utilities	604	0	1

[a]Married women generally employed as charwomen or in the laundry trade.
[b]Most women are employed as nurses and teachers (74%), or as
    clerks/administrators. There are 2 female doctors.
[c]Married women are employed here as innkeepers and boarding house keepers.
[d]One female painter/decorator is listed.
[e]Women employed in these trades are clerks and dealers.
[f]Women are employed as upholsterers.

Fig. 12.3: Male and Female Occupations in Plymouth and Devonport, 1911

Figure 12.3 shows details for the occupations held by men and women from the 1911 census. Although domestic service and the textiles trades still predominated, there was a larger range of occupations, including two female doctors. There is also an interesting split between the number of unmarried and married female workers: fifty per cent of unmarried women are employed compared to only eleven per cent of married/widowed women.

Both the First and Second World War brought immense changes to women's working lives and this is covered in more detail in chapter 18. But, particularly after the First World War, women were expected to go back to their pre-war roles. The return to domestic service was encouraged and vacancies advertised in the *WMN* of 17 January 1928, although including shorthand typists and a girl gardener, were still dominated by domestic service positions. However, the situation continued to change. On 10 July 1935 there were opportunities for a dental nurse, a lady clerk, a female carpet seamstress as well as saleswomen for a publishing house. On 29 November 1940, while many adverts still specified men, there were vacancies for jewellery saleswomen, a receptionist/bookkeeper for a hotel, a hotel manageress, nannies and housekeepers. By the 1950s there had been a dramatic shift from the domestic service and textiles industries to the clerical and hospitality sectors and adverts in the *WMN* of 1 November 1950 include teachers, a personal secretary, typists/telephonists, barmaids and hotel staff, with no mention of domestic service.

Further Reform

The Sex Disqualification (Removal) Act of 1919 meant women were no longer barred from civil or judicial office (including judge, barrister and solicitor) or from any profession. They could now become vets, accountants, surgeons and so on.[12] The Act did not, however, remove the marriage bar in certain industries and there were other limitations; restrictions could be made on admitting women to the civil service and women were barred from the foreign and diplomatic services until 1946.

In December 1933 the *WMN* reported on 'Careers for Women in the West' at a meeting chaired by Viscountess Bryce from the Central Employment Bureau for Women in London. She said that there were numerous different occupations a woman could now follow if she was trained and competent. Enquiries into the employment of women in Plymouth had found them in professions such as politics, limestone quarrying, timber merchants, medicine, massage, dentistry and journalism; a Miss Ormsby of Devonport was even studying marine engineering. Dr Mabel Ramsay told a reporter that there were not nearly enough women doctors to supply the demand and the agreement of the meeting was that:

> The capable and efficient woman can undertake practically every occupation if equal to the physical and nervous strain.

The marriage bar was removed from teaching and the BBC in 1944, the civil service in 1946 and the Foreign Office 1973. The general acceptance that married women did not work lingered long into the twentieth century. It was certainly expected that women would leave work when they had children and, as late as the 1970s, women could be sacked for becoming pregnant. The first maternity leave legislation was introduced by the 1975 Employment Protection Act, but because of the long qualifying period of employment a high proportion of women were not eligible and it wasn't until 1993 that coverage was extended to all women.

The provision of help with childcare was also a stumbling block for many women who wanted to work. In the nineteenth and early twentieth century women relied on relatives and neighbours and even their older children. Plymouth did make some provision – the Plymouth Day Nursery opened in April 1912 through a fund organised by the *Western Evening Herald* and the Astors opened the Francis and William Astor Nurseries in Plymouth and a day nursery in Devonport in 1917. During the Second World War the government recognised that mothers of young children needed childcare if they were to be able to do the work required by the country. Initial efforts encouraged women who were unable to take up war-work outside the home to provide childcare for those who could. These 'local guardians' were paid by both the mother and the state. In January 1942 the possibility of a wartime nursery in Plymouth was mooted but it was decided that the small demand for women's labour locally did not warrant one. By March however, the increasing number of working women meant the Ministry of Health considered Plymouth had a good case for the provision of one wartime nursery. By October the nursery was open at Hoe Street. Miss Crisp, the Women's Welfare Officer at the dockyard began to campaign for a second nursery at Devonport, providing evidence that thirty-five women had left due to domestic difficulties. By February 1943 the Ministry of Health was still reluctant to agree, stating that there were sufficient immobile women without children who could fill the labour demands. But in June 1943 this decision was reversed and a second nursery opened in August.

The Education Act of 1944 specified that local authorities should provide nursery provision for under 5s, giving women more opportunities to work and the women's liberation movement of the 1960s and 1970s ushered in an era of further campaign for equal pay and equal rights.

CHAPTER 13

Plymouth in Profile: Women on the Beat

'Girls come to us for advice, disputes are settled and fights have been stopped...'

From the start of the First World War, women's groups in Plymouth campaigned relentlessly for the appointment of female police officers in the face of considerable opposition.

At the start of twentieth century the extent of women's service in the police force was limited to constable's wives overseeing and searching female offenders. In 1914 the Plymouth Women's Co-operative Guild made representations for the appointment of female police but the *WMN* of 23 July 1914 reported the Watch Committee did not approve of the measure. The Plymouth branch of the National Union of Women Workers began voluntary patrols, but an application by them for the appointment of two part-time paid women police was declined again by the Watch Committee on 19 December 1917, although a police matron had been appointed to deal with juveniles and women detainees.

As the war progressed, other women's organisations joined the campaign. There was concern over the behaviour and safety of women given the increased number of servicemen in the town. The thrust of the campaign was for women to accompany patrols and give advice and guidance to young women who might find themselves in difficult situations. Finally, in May 1919, Plymouth Council resolved to appoint two policewomen and Inspector Carney and Policewoman Taylor were employed.

The women were involved mainly in rescue work with local women and had no powers of arrest.

On 14 January 1920 the Chief Constable of Plymouth reported to the Watch Committee that although initially he was 'not enamoured' of the appointment of the two women, they had proved themselves useful in the town and he hoped that the police force would be able to make more use of their services. Inspector Carney in her own report considered the work of the two women at Mill Street Fair most important – 'girls come to us for advice, disputes are settled and fights have been stopped'. Then, without warning, on 23 March 1921 the Watch Committee dismissed the two women.

Reports and letters to the local papers for some years afterwards record the controversy of this decision. Plymouth Citizens' Association protested strongly in the *WMN* of 30 March 1921, and on 18 April a letter to the editor from J Sandeman suggested that it would be beneficial for citizens to restart the women's patrols, which had done such excellent work at the start of the war. The Vice-President of the Plymouth Rotary Club had considered the two women a highly valuable social asset and thought they were dismissed for reasons that had nothing to do with their efficiency. He suggested that there was underhand play by the Watch Committee who passed the resolution to dismiss the women without full debate. As late as 1928 the issue was still being debated, and in October there was a letter from the PCA regarding evidence given to the Royal Commission on Police by Plymouth's Chief Constable on the subject. The PCA deeply regretted the tone of his evidence about the efficiency of the women and considered that the only reason for their dismissal was economic. All sections of the community had testified to their excellent work of and a petition had been signed by hundreds of women and mothers of girls who had been helped and 'set straight'.

The need for women police was continually raised in the local papers. Those who supported the idea stressed the benefits from a moral and social standpoint. Dr Mabel Ramsay, president of the PCA, suggested women police could patrol the parks and streets where young women and girls were in the habit of walking. In court they could take the statements of women. Both London and Birmingham had seen an increase in the number of women police and it was as important an issue in Plymouth.

But there was plenty of resistance. A letter to the editor of 18 November 1925 from a ratepayer protested against their employment and suggested that plain-clothes constables could do the job far better than any woman. On 20 November 1925, Mr L Dunstan (Chair of the Watch Committee when the two women were employed in 1919), wrote to say he had nothing but disdain for calls for women police and that the constant references to the immoral nature of Plymouth devalued the town. In his view, there were no problems and the cost would be a wanton waste of money.

The situation rumbled along with both sides standing firm to their viewpoint, but during the Second World War the subject rose to the forefront again. The Women's Auxiliary Police Corps (WAPC) was formed and women were appointed as clerks and telephonists to free up men for both war-work and patrols. But there were still no women police on patrol or with powers of arrest. Women's groups again began arranging meetings and protests, with Nancy Astor heavily involved. They highlighted the problems caused by the influx of serviceman – drinking, prostitution, home break-ups and the corruption of young girls and women. The *WMN* of 5 October 1943 reported from a meeting of the Standing Conference of Women's Organizations. They felt women were more likely to respond to, or share information with, female police officers and suggested that they:

> Were particularly needed to deal with girls as young as 14 who were running the streets ... at funfairs, camps and every other building where servicemen were to be found.

At a meeting of the Watch Committee in August 1943 the Chief Constable said that:

> While of course young girls should be protected from the
> risks of low morality, he felt there was some ignorance
> over the power the police had in dealing with such
> problems – they were not moral welfare workers. He did
> not want to say that women's help was not valued by the
> police. In cases of youngsters exposed to moral danger
> then police matrons ... and members of the Auxiliary
> Police Corps were frequently employed. But morals
> were the duty of religious and welfare organisations.

Campaigning continued. In the *Western Evening Herald* of
4 November 1943, Lady Astor reported that she had asked
the Home Office whether it was time to make employment of
women police compulsory for all local authorities. The reply
was that it would be going too far to compel appointments,
but it was the policy of the Home Office to encourage their
employment if suitable women could be found.

But the Watch Committee was stubborn. By December
1943 the Home Office had intimated to Plymouth that it would
approve the appointment of suitable women from the WAPC
for uniformed patrol. Six women over and above the normal
force could be appointed and this would mean no reduction in
male officers. Despite this encouragement the Watch Committee
turned down the proposal by a majority of one.

In April 1944, the tide began to turn. The Standing
Committee of Women's Organizations wrote to the Watch
Committee to say they believed the Home Secretary was about
to take action to deal with the problem in Plymouth. They
suggested that it would be better if the city could appoint women
police voluntarily before being directed to do so. Finally, in
June 1944, the *WMN* reported that the Watch Committee had
approved the appointment of women police. The committee
went on to say that:

> This did not mean that the Watch had 'changed its
> mind' nor was it a 'volte-face' on their part but rather
> a response to meet a request from headquarters and

action to meet an emergency. It should be regarded as a war-time measure only.

Despite the 'war-time measure only' statement, at the end of the war three of the six women were offered permanent employment and Plymouth finally had its women police.

CHAPTER 14

Public and Community Life

'A woman is absolutely disqualified by nature from being elected...'

Women gained the right to vote in, and stand for, elections to local councils, school boards and Boards of Guardians significantly earlier than they achieved the parliamentary vote, but the road to the local franchise was paved with similar prejudices and obstacles.

The 1869 Municipal Franchise Act gave the local vote to qualified women, but the situation was complicated. In 1872 the High Court ruled that married women could not vote as they had no legal identity separate from their husbands, and in 1880 a court of appeal case ruled that women could not stand for election with the words: 'a woman is absolutely disqualified by nature from being elected'.[1]

The 1894 Local Government Act finally clarified that all women, irrespective of their marital status, had the right to vote in, and to stand for, election on parish councils, district councils, school boards and Boards of Guardians. Election of women onto Borough and County Councils came with the 1907 Qualification of Women (County and Borough Councils) Act.

Local Government

On 12 September 1919, Dr Mabel Ramsay wrote to the *WMN* in support of three independent female candidates put forward by the Plymouth Citizens' Association to stand in the forthcoming council elections. The PCA promised to support any women, whether independent or party-affiliated. The Labour

1869	Municipal Franchise Act: qualified women are able to vote in local elections
1871	First School Board forms in Plymouth
1872	The High Court rules that married women are disqualified from voting in municipal elections as they have no separate identity
1880	Court of Appeal rules that women cannot stand for local elections
1892	Miss Spooner first woman elected onto Plymouth School Board
1894	Local Government Act: establishes that all women can vote in or stand for local elections
1902	Education Act dissolves School Boards
1907	Qualification of Women Act: women can stand for election on to Borough and County Councils
1918	Parliament (Qualification of Women) Act: women can stand for parliamentary elections
1919	Mrs Daymond and Mrs Simpson first women to be elected on to Plymouth City Council
1922	Mrs Daymond elected Chair of Devonport Board of Guardians
1929	Local Government Act dissolves Boards of Guardians
1950	Jacquetta Marshall elected first female Lord Mayor of Plymouth

Fig. 14.1: Timeline of Municipal Election Legislation

Co-operative also put forward a female candidate. The election results were announced on 3 November with Mrs Daymond (Independent) and Mrs Simpson (Labour) securing the first victories for women and a large gathering of women supporters received the announcement with much enthusiasm. Miss Bayly, although initially defeated, won a by-election a few weeks later after the death of the incumbent.

Over the ensuing years, a handful of women continued to stand at local elections with some success but the increase of female members of the council was slow. In 1925, Mrs Jacquetta Marshall was the only successful woman candidate and by 1950 there were still few female councillors. Jacquetta Marshall was the first female Mayor of Plymouth and in an article in the *WMN* of 6 October 1950 she recalled the suffrage meetings she used to attend in the firm belief that all women should have the vote. She was a Poor Law Guardian from 1922 until the Board was dissolved in 1930 and was instrumental in changing the school uniform for those children who lived in scattered homes – doing away with the capes and straw hats which singled them out. In 1925 she stood as a Labour candidate and was elected onto Plymouth City Council for Sutton Ward, becoming the first female alderman in 1927. Her particular interests lay in children and the sick and she was a member of hospital and welfare committees as well as the Women's Co-operative Guild where she began to learn the art of public speaking. In March 1950 she was nominated for the office of Lord Mayor. When she donned her new lightweight robes and featherless tricorn hat, she said that she felt it was 'the woman, the housewife and the family who were being particularly honoured'. She was awarded an OBE in 1955.

Boards of Guardians and School Boards

In the *WDM* of 10 January 1889 a 'Lady Poor Law Guardian' reported on the importance of women becoming involved in Boards of Guardians. Of around 20,000 guardians, only fifty-eight were female. Many of the duties called for the same qualities of knowledge and observation as in the management of any domestic house. Of the inmates at least four-fifths were women and children and officers of the workhouses (themselves largely female) said that:

> There are many things we could speak of better to a lady and which naturally come under a woman's province such as diet and laundry and the control of the many sad cases of women and girls in the workhouse.

She thought that perhaps the interests of the inmates would have been better cared for if women had been able to exert their influence in the past.

There was opposition to the idea of female guardians. In 1893 Stonehouse Board of Guardians agreed that ladies should be given the authority to visit the workhouse but there was general agreement that lady guardians were not necessary. Concerns were that women were over-inquisitive, would be inclined to overspend on the budget and should not be involved in immoral discussions regarding unmarried mothers and prostitutes.

In support of female guardians, Miss Garland from Plymouth addressed the Exeter and District Women's Liberal Association in October 1894. She echoed the view that many of the duties of the guardians were highly suited to women and that women were far more economical spenders. To the laughter which followed, she challenged any man to take on the housekeeping money and make it stretch as far as his wife did.

Plymouth did elect female guardians as early as 1892, but their presence was a source of some friction. The *WMN* of 13 September 1893 reported on a meeting of the board which included four women – Mrs Ripley, Miss Fox, Miss Spooner and Miss Spearman. A discussion over the workhouse doctor's authority to prescribe alcohol to inmates for medicinal purposes, to which Mrs Ripley was strongly against, ended with a male guardian remarking that:

> The discussion had been going on for so long it was
> a question of which had become more stale, Mrs Ripley
> or the ale.

By January 1895 none of the female guardians had been re-elected. There had been controversy when the workhouse children had not been allowed to attend a pantomime due to the atmosphere of debauchery and drunkenness they would have encountered. Miss Spooner explained that alternative entertainment had been provided which they had thoroughly enjoyed, but much anger had been directed at the lady guardians. She did not, however, think this was the sole reason for their non-election, as the men who had equally objected to the pantomime were still voted in. Rather, she attributed it to the persistent way in which some of the male guardians opposed women being there at all, arguing that many of the deliberations were too improper, a view unfortunately echoed by many of the voters. Nevertheless, she was proud of the three years she had spent on the board. Another suggestion for the lack of success of the Plymouth lady guardians was that they had all been strong temperance supporters, whereas the drink trade had a loud and influential voice in the town. The one lady guardian at Devonport was connected with the drink trade, which seemed most suspicious. The *Englishman's Review* of 1895 listed the recent elections and appointments of women which were double that of any previous years but Plymouth had gained an unenviable notoriety for being the only town where lady guardians were not re-elected.

But the women were nothing if not persistent. Over the years they were returned to the board and their presence became more acceptable. In April 1922, Mrs Clara Daymond was unanimously elected Chair of the Devonport Guardians, the first woman to preside over the board and in April 1923 Mrs Wyatt was elected as governor of the Plymouth board, having spent a year as treasurer.

The 1929 Local Government Act dissolved the Boards of Guardians and responsibilities for the poor were passed to

A LADY GUARDIAN.

MRS. WYATT ELECTED UNOPPOSED AT PLYMOUTH.

Mrs. Wyatt, of 5, St. James-place East, has been returned unopposed as Guardian for Hoe Ward, Plymouth, to fill the vacancy caused by the retirement of Mr. F. C. H. Harvey. No other candidate was nominated.

Election of a Lady Poor Law Guardian at Plymouth, 3 June 1912. (Western Morning News)

local authorities. In the *WMN* of 28 March 1930, 'Women in the West' reminisced over the years of the guardians and reflected on how strange it was that once there had been no women on the boards, given how necessary their help had proven to be.

Women were eligible to stand on school boards created by the 1870 Education Act. Plymouth's first school board formed in 1871, but it wasn't until 1892 that a woman was elected. The *WMN* of 13 January 1892 recorded that of eighteen candidates nominated for the upcoming elections, a woman, schoolmistress Miss Agnes Spooner, was standing for election for the first time. She had been nominated by Isaac Foot and Reverend Binns, both of whom were staunch supporters of women's rights. Miss Spooner was successful and remained on the board for several years. However the 1902 Education Act dissolved school boards and passed control to local education authorities. At this time, women were far less likely to be serving on local councils and therefore their influence over the running of schools was diminished for a time.

Community Action

Women were involved in a variety of organisations, both national and local. They organised public meetings and lectures, supported local politicians and fundraised for a range of causes. Meetings ranged from large public gatherings to more intimate 'at-homes'. The Three Towns had a number of such organisations:

The Women's Co-operative Guild formed in 1883 to promote women's rights and support suffrage, with particular interest in the welfare and education of working-class women. A Plymouth branch opened in the 1880s which was involved in many campaigns in the town including the appointment of women police.

Plymouth Citizens' Association was inaugurated on 2 June 1919, following the partial enfranchisement of women in 1918. The Association was open to both men and women and supported not only the push for equal franchise, but many other issues affecting women and the local community. In June 1922 at the PCA annual meeting, an ambitious programme was revealed which aimed to secure:

- The return of women police
- The appointment of women magistrates
- The adequate representation of women in the affairs of the community, with their presence on all governing bodies and other areas where their assistance would be beneficial
- An adequately equipped and modern maternity hospital
- The franchise on equal terms with men

The association ran for several more years after the Equal Franchise Act of 1928. It had several successes, including the appointment of female magistrates and police officers.

Townswomen's Guild: The *WMN* of 21 March 1933 reported that, although only recently formed, the Plymouth Townswomen's Guild was already doing useful work. The first Townswomen's Guild was formed in Haywards Heath in 1929 with the aim of educating women about good citizenship in the

9th Devonport St Mary's Girl Guides. (South West Image Bank)

wake of the 1928 Equal Franchise Act, but they also offered a range of educational and social activities. In November 1936 at the second annual dinner of the Guild, Mrs J Buller Kitson expressed her pride in the involvement of the group in civic affairs. The need for more women councillors was discussed as was the requirement for more women on the bench. Townswomen's Guilds are still active all over the country with four branches currently in Plymouth.

Girl Guides: On 8 May 1917 Mrs Astor called a meeting to consider the extension of the Girl Guide movement to Plymouth. She considered training in the Guides to be immensely beneficial – it quickened intelligence, made girls resourceful and responsible and gave them discipline and self-respect. It brought all classes together, was non-political and non-denominational, and taught the girls numerous skills. Enthusiasm spread and local schools and societies formed companies. In July 1917 Mrs Astor visited the Paradise Road School in Stoke to inspect their Girl Guides and was pleased to learn that there were two companies, Brownies for girls age 8–11, and Guides for those over 11. At a meeting of the Plymouth Girl Guides Association in September that year it was reported that over 1,100 girls had enrolled throughout Plymouth.

Women's Liberal Association: During the late nineteenth century, political parties began to recognise the persuasiveness that women could bring to canvassing and public speaking. The Women's Liberal Association first formed in Bristol and branches opened locally in the Three Towns. In 1884 the *WMN* reported the first gathering of the WLA at the Borough Arms Coffee Tavern. The chair was Frances Latimer, daughter of the president of the Plymouth Liberal Association. Miss Latimer was an advocate of female suffrage and she introduced a weekly letter to the *Western Daily Mercury* on women's issues.

The Conservatives had an equivalent, the Primrose League, but while the Primrose League ladies were not specifically concerned with women's issues, the WLA from the outset maintained that women should be involved in political life and processes. In April 1893 there was a Conference of the Southern Counties Women's Liberal Association Union at Plymouth. The conference considered matters of vital interest to women, including the role of women and children in factories, separation orders and custody of children, the abolishment of capital punishment and anti-vivisection. They also discussed again the necessity of women having the vote and it was agreed that the WLA would not support any Liberal candidate opposed to women's suffrage, showing their policy of women before party.

The late nineteenth and early twentieth century saw an increase in the participation of women in public life, although it was not really until the interwar years that their presence in local government became more prevalent. The opportunities open to women strengthened the role they were playing and allowed them to gain valuable experience in campaigning, debating and implementing policies; they were able to build support networks with likeminded men and women. Although the roles tended to be restricted to the middle classes, they were perhaps given a better insight into the hardships the poorer classes faced. It is interesting to note the same names cropping up in the Three Towns: Clara Daymond was elected to Boards of Guardians and the local council, Miss Spooner was on both Plymouth Board of Guardians and school board, Miss Bayly was a local councillor and magistrate. The determination of these women and their dedication to both women's causes and the local community is clear. There has been some comment that the women who first found themselves in public office were only concerned with 'women's issues' such as children, poverty, schooling and health. But perhaps this is the point. Emmeline Pankhurst became a Poor Law Guardian in 1895 and the horrors of what she encountered in the workhouse – young children scrubbing floors in the depths of winter, elderly inmates with no privacy and no belongings, unmarried mothers with no home – cemented her determination that women must have the vote. These were the issues which women felt were ignored and these were the people who would have no voice in government until women were able to influence policy.

CHAPTER 15

Women in Profile: Nancy Astor

'The worst of it is, the woman is sure to get in...'

Born in 1879 in Virginia, USA, Nancy Langhorne travelled to England in 1905 and married Waldorf Astor. In 1910, Waldorf Astor was elected as one of Plymouth's two MPs, but succeeded to his father's title in 1919. As a member of the House of Lords he had to relinquish his Plymouth Sutton seat, triggering a by-election. The 1918 Parliament (Qualification of Women) Act allowed women to stand for Parliament and Nancy stood in the by-election in her husband's place, as a Unionist candidate. Many had reservations, including the party chairman, Sir George Younger, who said: 'The worst of it is, the woman is sure to get in.' She did, winning with a fifty-one per cent share of the vote and a majority of over 5,000. Her campaign had been an active one and she had shown her ability to orate and to deal with hecklers with wit and charm. She also moderated her strong views on temperance and used women's meetings to gain the support of newly enfranchised female voters. She took her seat on 1 December 1919, the first female Member of Parliament in British history to do so. (The Irish Republican Countess Constance Markievicz became the first elected female MP for Sinn Fein but did not take her seat.) That evening Nancy gave a dinner party in the House of Commons to which the prime minister, David Lloyd George, his ministers and many other MPs were invited.

Her maiden speech was given on 24 February 1920 and the House of Commons was packed, partly due to the prime minister making an important announcement on foreign policy, but also in no small part due to Nancy's reputation as a wit and

"DAILY MIRROR'S" PLAN TO HELP EX-OFFICERS

The Daily Mirror

CERTIFIED CIRCULATION LARGER THAN THAT OF ANY OTHER DAILY PICTURE PAPER

No. 5,021. SATURDAY, NOVEMBER 29, 1919 [16 PAGES.] One Penny.

PLYMOUTH ELECTS LADY ASTOR: FIRST WOMAN M.P.

The Hon. Esmond Harmsworth, who has won a splendid victory.

Viscount Astor, husband of the new M.P. His elevation to the peerage created the vacancy.

Captain W. J. West, the defeated Isle of Thanet Liberal.

A studio portrait of Viscountess Astor, the first woman M.P.

Viscountess Astor addressing a meeting. Hecklers had to be careful, for she has a ready repartee.

Group showing Viscountess Astor with her children. She is an American and one of the four beautiful Langhorne sisters.

Viscountess Astor makes a megaphone with her hands. She worked untiringly during the election campaign.

The electors of the Sutton Division of Plymouth have made history by returning Viscountess Astor as their M.P. The result of the poll was announced yesterday, the figures being received with the greatest enthusiasm, and when the new member appeared on the balcony with her little son "Billy" she tried to make a speech, but her voice was drowned by the cheers. The result of the Isle of Thanet election was also announced yesterday, the figures showing a majority of 2,633 votes for the Hon. Esmond Harmsworth, the first anti-waste candidate to be returned. The Liberal nominee was Captain W. J. West.

Newspaper Report of the Election of Nancy Astor, 1919. (Mary Evans Picture Library)

perhaps to see the novelty of a woman speaking to an audience of over 500 men. She referred to her election and said:

> Honourable Members should not be frightened of what Plymouth sends out into the world ... I would like to

say that I am quite certain that the women of the whole world will not forget that it was the fighting men of Devon who dared to send the first woman to represent women in the Mother of Parliaments.[1]

The bulk of her speech was on the perils of drink as part of a debate on removing drinking restrictions that had been introduced during the First World War. She was concerned that their removal could have an adverse effect on women and children. She reminded the House that during the war the convictions of drunkenness among women was one-fifth of what it had been, and this at a time when women were earning their own wage and were under enormous physical and mental strain. Since the restrictions had been only slightly modified, the convictions among women had already doubled. She told of seeing a child of around 5 waiting for its mother outside of a pub in Plymouth. When the mother eventually 'reeled' out the child went to her but then retreated:

> Oh the oaths and curses of that poor woman and the shrieks of the child as it fled from her. That is what goes on when you have increased drunkenness among women. I am thinking of the women and children.[2]

In 1923 she introduced a Private Member's Bill which led to the prohibition of the sale of alcohol to under 18s.

Although she had no links with the early suffrage campaign, she was a passionate advocate of women's equality and rights. In her maiden speech to Parliament she referred to the fact that some women over 30 could now vote saying: 'women have got a vote now and we mean to use it, and to use it wisely.' She supported the campaign for equal suffrage which resulted in the Equal Franchise Act of 1928. She was a keen supporter of educational reform and advocated the development of nursery schools. In 1912 the Astors funded two nurseries, one on Whimple Street for poor working women and the Francis Astor Day nursery on Cecil Street, and others followed. She worked tirelessly in Plymouth on various bodies and organisations and on issues

Young Supporter of Nancy Astor.
(South West Image Bank)

such as the recruitment of women into the civil service and the police force, maternal mortality and birth control clinics.

Her life was nothing if not controversial. Oswald Mosley supported her during her election campaign in 1919 and in the 1930s, as part of the 'Cliveden Set', she was notorious for being sympathetic to Germany over its treatment after the First World War. Both she and Waldorf Astor initially objected to engaging in the Second World War, supporting Neville Chamberlain and his policy of appeasement. However, in the early stages of the war, she voted against the government, helping Winston Churchill to become prime minister and throughout the war she devoted a great deal of time to raising morale in Plymouth, which was devastated during the Blitz, apparently performing cartwheels and leading dances on the Hoe.

She is credited with a number of quotes which show her quick wit. In response to the congratulations on being elected to Parliament and her admission to 'the most exclusive men's club in Europe' she is said to have replied, 'It won't be exclusive for long. When I came in I left the door wide open!' She is also rumoured to have had a particularly volatile relationship with Churchill, but sadly the oft-quoted exchange between them:

Elliott Terrace – Plymouth home of the Astors. (Chris Glasspool)

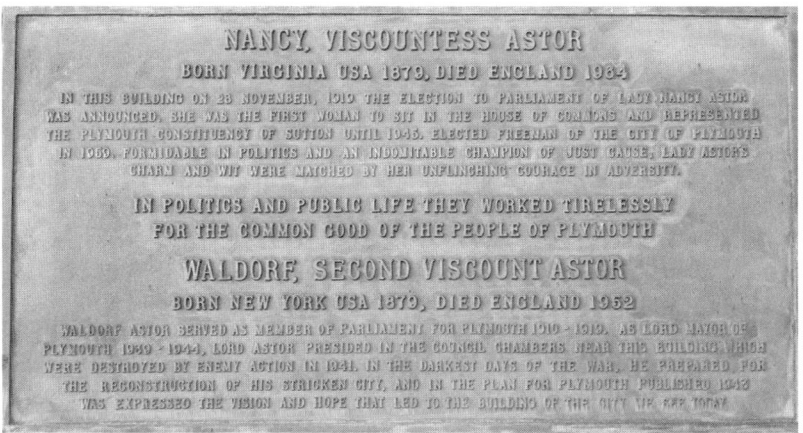

Astor Plaque on Guildhall, Plymouth. (Chris Glasspool)

Nancy: 'Sir, if you were my husband I'd poison your coffee,'

Churchill: 'Madam, if you were my wife I'd drink it,'

is believed to be a myth.

Nancy was MP for Plymouth for twenty-six years, being returned in a further six elections. She reluctantly stood down in 1945 on the advice of both her husband and the Conservative party who felt that she was becoming too erratic and outspoken in her views and a liability to the party. When she first took her seat she was the only female MP for almost two years. When she left, twenty-four women MPs had taken their seats and the Plymouth Sutton seat from which she stood down was immediately won by another woman, Lucy Middleton. In 1959, Nancy was made an Honorary Freeman of the City of Plymouth. In the same year she launched HMS *Plymouth*, and presented the city with a diamond and sapphire necklace to be worn by the Lady Mayoress. The Astors were generous with their fortune, giving buildings, land and money to the city, including 3 Elliot Terrace, which became the official residence of the Lord Mayor and is now accommodation for official visitors.

Nancy Astor died at the home of her daughter in 1964 at the age of 84.

MP	Party	Ward	Dates Served
Lady Nancy Astor	Unionist	Plymouth Sutton	1919–45
Lucy Middleton	Labour	Plymouth Sutton	1945–51
Dame Joan Vickers	Conservative	Plymouth Devonport	1955–74
Dame Janet Fookes	Conservative	Plymouth Drake	1974–97
Linda Gilroy	Labour	Plymouth Sutton	1997–2010
Alison Seabeck	Labour	Plymouth Devonport	2005–10
Alison Seabeck	Labour	Plymouth Moor View	2010–15

Fig. 15.1: Plymouth's Female MPs

CHAPTER 16

Leisure and Lifestyle

'I do not know what I do. I stay about the house...'

Class Barriers to Leisure

Working Class Wives, published in 1930, surveyed the health of working-class women and included questions on leisure activities. The results showed that many working-class women had neither the time nor the money for leisure, sometimes not even suitable footwear or clothing for anything other than walking to the local shops. One woman with a family of six young children and an uncooperative husband responded:

> I do not know what I do. I stay about the house, sometimes, but not often, I take the children for a walk but I haven't any outdoor clothes so I chat to neighbours … and sit on the back step mending and darning.

Working Class Wives is full of such accounts of women whose days were spent cooking and cleaning and who rarely had any time to themselves. One woman even propped a copy of Longfellow on her washtub so she could read while doing laundry. It was not really until the advent of cheap matinee performances at cinemas during the interwar years, and the more prevalent use of labour-saving devices after the Second World War, that working-class women began to really have – and make use of – leisure time. Even the simple advent of the wireless was a boon to them with the number increasing from 200,000 in 1923 to over 8.5 million in 1939.

Ladies at the Palace Theatre, Plymouth c.1920s. (South West Image Bank)

In contrast, the middle and upper classes had both time and resources. Their leisure time could be filled with trips to cinemas and theatres, attending meetings and lectures and

Announcements, &c.

THEATRE ROYAL, PLYMOUTH.

Lessee and Manager ..... Mr. C. F. WILLIAMS.
Acting Manager .... Mr. J. LANGDON LEE.

TO-NIGHT AT 7.30.

EARLY DOORS, 6.45; ORDINARY, 7.15.

MR. HENRY DUNDAS AND COMPANY IN THE GREAT
DRURY LANE DRAMA.

"HUMAN NATURE."

"HUMAN NATURE."

MONDAY NEXT, SEPTEMBER 5TH,
FIRST VISIT TO PLYMOUTH OF ENGLAND'S
GREATEST ACTRESS,

MISS ELLEN TERRY,

AND COMPANY.
MONDAY AND TUESDAY,
"THE MERCHANT OF VENICE."

WEDNESDAY, THURSDAY, AND FRIDAY,
"MUCH ADO ABOUT NOTHING."

SATURDAY MATINEE,
"THE MERCHANT OF VENICE."

SATURDAY NIGHT,
"THE GOOD HOPE."

NOTICE.

TO AVOID DISAPPOINTMENT SEATS SHOULD BE BOOKED
AS EARLY AS POSSIBLE.

DRESS CIRCLE AND ORCHESTRA STALLS, 5s.

Box Plan now open at the Theatre from 10 a.m. to 4 p.m.
(Tele. 196); Messrs. SWISS and CO., Fore-street, Devonport
(Tele. 43).

The Theatre Royal, Plymouth, September 1904. (Western Morning News)

CRITERION KINEMA,
CORNWALL-STREET (Close to George-street).
FOR 'SIX DAYS ONLY.
TIMES OF SHOWING, 2.45, 5.45, 8.50.
THE PERFECT PHOTOPLAY!
EXQUISITE IN ITS DAINTY
WHOLESOME CONCEPTION.
"SMILIN' THROUGH,"
With NORMA TALMADGE,
the Greatest Masterpiece of Silent Art ever given to the Screen. It is a revelation in every way. Charged with the emotions of all mankind, it tells of wonderful parallel loves— loves of to-day and yesterday, of youth supreme, hope eternal, and love undying— love that rises above the Vale of Heartbreak to come "SMILIN' THROUGH" the Gates of Gladness.
THE DRAMA STUPENDOUS
EXCLUSIVELY PRESENTED AT
CRITERION KINEMA
Certainly Plymouth's Biggest Attraction This Week. Seats can be Booked for Matinées.

Advert for the Criterion Kinema, November 1922. (Western Morning News)

sporting activities. The Three Towns had a number of theatres and music halls.

On 20 September 1910 the *WMN* advertised a variety show at the Palace Theatre to include a violinist; a Japanese juggler; cycling monkeys; gymnasts; Amy Anderson & Co in 'The Banana Queen'; an acrobat; a comedian and singer/dancer Marie Kay. Music Hall stars who played in Plymouth included Marie Lloyd, Lillie Langtry and Adelaide Hall.

The first 'picture palaces' began to open in Plymouth at the start of the twentieth century and on 21 July 1910 the *WMN* reported that the Watch Committee had granted licences under the 1909 Cinematograph Act to Andrews Picture Palace, Union Street and the Belgrave Hall, Mutley. On 16 August it was reported that Andrews Picture Palace had been well patronised and had a varied programme, an orchestra and realistic sound effects and a guide who announced and described the pictures when necessary. Films had included the 'Cowes Regatta' and 'Rubber and pepper growing in Malay.'

Fickle Fashions

Changes in clothing styles and fashions over the decades, with eventual freedom from restrictive and controlling modes of dress, echoed the freedoms women were experiencing in other areas of their lives.

Until the end of the nineteenth century, women's clothing was heavy and restrictive. Long, full skirts, bustles and corsets predominated, trapping women in layers of clothing which they needed assistance to get into and out of. Heavy clothing was even the cause of a number of deaths by drowning. Such fashions did have other uses though – the *Western Courier* of 4 September 1850 reported that two women were arrested at Plymouth for smuggling when they arrived on a cutter from Jersey. When searched they were found to have 32lbs of cut tobacco between them, concealed in their bustles.

As today, the newspapers contained columns devoted to following the latest fashions from Paris and London. In the *Western Courier* of 2 May 1850, Mrs Bull's Mantle and Millinery Showrooms of 26 George Street, Plymouth were advertised, 'replete with every novelty of the season'. Beauty products were also advertised. The *Western Courier* of 21 May 1851 had a range including Rondeletia soap for softening and beautifying the skin, Oriental Oil to promote hair growth and, particularly important in Plymouth, to 'correct the pernicious effects of sea bathing'.

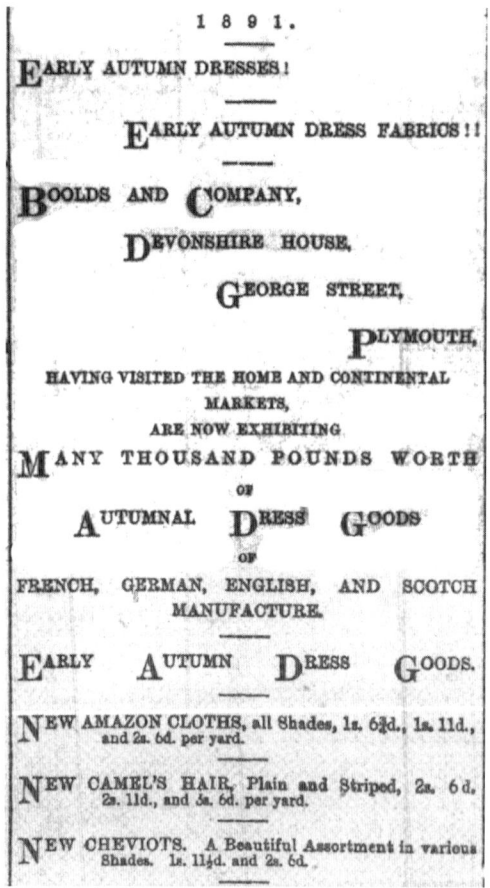

1 8 9 1.

EARLY AUTUMN DRESSES!

EARLY AUTUMN DRESS FABRICS!!

BOOLDS AND COMPANY,

DEVONSHIRE HOUSE,

GEORGE STREET,

PLYMOUTH,

HAVING VISITED THE HOME AND CONTINENTAL
MARKETS,
ARE NOW EXHIBITING

MANY THOUSAND POUNDS WORTH

OF

AUTUMNAL DRESS GOODS

OF

FRENCH, GERMAN, ENGLISH, AND SCOTCH
MANUFACTURE.

EARLY AUTUMN DRESS GOODS.

NEW AMAZON CLOTHS, all Shades, 1s. 6¾d., 1s. 11d.,
and 2s. 6d. per yard.

NEW CAMEL'S HAIR, Plain and Striped, 2s. 6d.
2s. 11d., and 3s. 6d. per yard.

NEW CHEVIOTS. A Beautiful Assortment in various
Shades. 1s. 11½d. and 2s. 6d.

Boolds Fashions, October 1891.
(Western Morning News)

In the early 1880s, protest against the discomfort of women's clothing saw the formation of the Rational Dress Society under the presidency of Viscountess Halberton. The *WMN* of 30 May 1881 reported the society's aims:

The desire is to release women from the tyranny of fashion and to allow them to dress with the condition that attire should be both pleasing to the eye and conform to the considerations of health and comfort.

The Rational Dress Society promoted the 'divided skirt' – a pair of trousers worn under a long coat or 'riding-habit' style of garment. On 12 October 1881 a writer in the *WMN* reported on seeing two ladies wearing such an item. He thought there was nothing objectionable about the garment and it must contribute to freedom of movement and comfort. However, an article of 25 September 1882 reported that 'the divided skirt has been roundly rejected', and it does appear that it failed to gain the support that the Society had been hoping for. However, the fashion for cycling which came about towards the end of the century raised its profile again and in the *WMN* of 20 June 1888, the West Riding Association suggested that the substitution of rational dress would be a great advantage for cycling given the danger and discomfort of cycling in skirts. The report concluded that:

> Should a woman appear dressed in crinoline and poke bonnet she would today cause more consternation than a rationally-clad cyclist.

But while the craze for cycling helped the cause, it was the First World War which really galvanised the change in what was acceptable attire for women. The women who became involved in war-work adopted much more practical

PERMANENT WAVING.

Have your Hair Waved for Xmas.

Special Terms for December.

Full Head	...	£2 2 0
Half ,,	...	1 10 0
Side piece	...	10 6

The very latest Model Machines.
London trained Operators.
Best service in Town at Lowest Prices.
Call, Write, or Phone, and book at once.

WRIGHT

(Established 65 years),

HAIRDRESSER.

Union Street. Plymouth.

Have Your Hair Waved for Christmas, December 1926. (Western Morning News)

1920s Fashions. (South West Image Bank)

clothing. Overalls, uniforms and trousers were all worn for both ease and comfort and this paved the way for the more drastic changes of the 1920s – the era of the short bob, the cloche hat and the flapper.

A sun-tan was also emphasised for the first time, although this was as fickle as all fashions. In the *WMN* of 28 August 1930 it was reported that, although the vogue *had* been for tanned skin:

> Paris had decreed a cream and roses complexion for the coming winter and many a girl on return to town after the summer season would be looking for ways to pale her skin. As those who holidayed at home had not seen much sun, then for once the business girl would mark that as a score against her more leisured sisters.

On 7 July 1930 the *WMN* suggested that women hesitating over whether to welcome or resent the return of long dresses might be helped by a note in 'Better Health', the publication of the Plymouth Public Health Department, which suggested that short dresses and light clothing had done more for women's health and happiness than any other reform. Rather condescendingly though, the article concludes that doctors should address their concerns to the fashion dictators of London and Paris as 'women had no will of their own in such matters'.

An article in the *WMN* of 18 October 1939 reflected on the differences of fashions of the day compared to those of twenty-five years previously. It paid tribute to those whose change of attire during the First World War resulted in:

> Some very futuristic young ladies now even wearing a modified form of trousers called 'dungarees'. Those ladies who were seen in public in the land army uniform of breeches, open-necked shirts and brogues were brave indeed and the modern ambulance drivers of today who unconcernedly wear slacks are indebted to those pioneers.

Mixed tennis group, 1920s. (South West Image Bank)

The Second World War brought fabric shortages and the era of make-do-and-mend. In 1947 Christian Dior introduced the 'New Look', with fuller skirts and cinched waists, which continued into the 1950s. The final nail in the coffin of restricted dress came with the swinging sixties, and although to some extent fashion still dictates what both women and men wear, there is no sign of any return to the restrictive rules of the past.

Sports and Swimming

Despite the claims of some quarters over the inappropriateness of physical activity for women, they took part in a number of sports including tennis, golf, hockey and cycling. In the *WMN* of 20 December 1895 an 'active woman' described a new mechanical toy – 'a lady cyclist who blows kisses as she rides'. The writer considered this rather an aspersion of flippancy on the character of lady cyclists! In the *WMN* of February 1936 there were details of an exercise class from Miss Prunella Stack of the Women's Health and Beauty League. The object of the League was to promote health and beauty with exercises which

Lady golfer 1920s. (South West Image Bank)

developed physique. Teachers were all trained in anatomy and exercises were scientific and performed to music to ensure swing, rhythm and suppleness.

Swimming and sea bathing was a particular interest for the women of Plymouth and does not seem to have aroused the same consternation that other sports sometimes did, although men's and women's bathing was strictly segregated for some time.

A Ladies Bathing Place was established in Plymouth by the mid-nineteenth century. The *WMN* of 25 August 1881 reported on how popular swimming had become among Plymouth ladies and, to encourage girls and young children, matches were being held at the Ladies Bathing Place under the Hoe. All girls who completed the course were given a prize and many showed a fine swimming style, while all others needed was a little practice. In June 1883, Madam Gent advertised her ladies' swimming lessons and in July 1887 the Mermaid Bathing and Swimming Club for ladies was proposed, to consist of a vessel moored off the Hoe with two spacious floating baths for non-swimmers and children. This was operating in 1889 along with several clubs for men.

Lady swimmers under Plymouth Pier, 1920s. (South West Image Bank)

Swimmers at Tinside Lido, 1920s. (South West Image Bank)

There were also complaints of men and youths bathing in a state of nudity between the Ladies Bathing Place and West Hoe Pier.

Bathing houses at Tinside beach on the Hoe were formally opened as Tinside Lido in August 1913 and over the years this was developed further. In 1918, the Hoe and Parks Committee of Plymouth Council resolved to fix notices at the men's bathing places warning them to stop using the ladies' bathing raft. This was raised again at a meeting on 22 April 1918 and it was agreed that notices should also be fixed to the actual raft in the hope that this would be more of a deterrent.

Swimming competitions for both men and women were a regular event and the *WMN* of 22 September 1919 reported that Violet Manley had won the Western Counties Ladies Amateur Championship – the first time the prize had been brought back to Devon. Miss Manley first began swimming in 1909, and in 1912 she joined the Port of Plymouth (Ladies Branch) Swimming Association. The Plymouth Ladies Swimming Association was formed in 1920/21 with a clubroom on the Promenade Pier, and on 27 May 1929 was still going strong with a report of fifty members opening the season by taking their first dip of the year. Mrs Jessie Boultwood, Captain of the Plymouth Ladies Football Club, was also Captain of the Plymouth Ladies Swimming Club and winner of the Port of Plymouth Swimming Championships. Tinside Lido fell into disuse in the 1980s and closed in 1992 but was developed and reopened in 2003.

CHAPTER 17

Plymouth in Profile: Plymouth's Lady Footballers

'Football is quite unsuitable for females...'

Women were playing football in the 1890s, with Preston's Dick Kerr Ladies formed in 1894, but it was during the First World War that the game spread. Women working in munitions factories began to form teams and the game both reinforced the image of women's war work and was a good fundraiser for wartime charities.

At the end of the war many women's teams disbanded, but, despite the bemusement and outright hostility of many, some carried on and continued to attract large crowds. The 'Plymouth Ladies' were no exception and local newspapers printed match reports and letters from those keen to critique the games. In April 1921, 'A Male Admirer of Pluck' praised the game. He considered it to be no more harmful than cycling and ended by offering his services in coaching. Others were not so complimentary. A letter of December 1921 from 'JD' says:

> I saw a football match (?) between the Plymouth 'Ladies' and the Marazion 'Ladies' some weeks ago and I can only say that I hope it will not be my fate to sit out another. The term 'Ladies' does not seem to apply at all.

It is not clear whether JD objects to the state of play or the demeanour of the 'Ladies'.

Plymouth was a well-organised team and they had a string of fixtures throughout 1921. They were coached by Frank Zanazzi, an experienced physical training instructor who held training sessions on the beach, including javelin throwing and hurdling as well as the more usual fitness training. On 29 April they beat Bath City 2–0 in front of a large crowd and the Plymothians were reported as showing good form in an interesting game. In May the Plymouth Ladies entertained a French international side at Home Park in front of a crowd of 11,000. They lost the match 1–0 but the newspaper reported:

> Not much more could have been expected of a side who had only formed twelve weeks before and they played a good game and with practice ought to be a capable side.

The report went on to praise the French team for their quickness on the ball and more polished methods, going so far as to say that 'some of the movements would have done credit to a good league team'. On 1 June, Plymouth beat Newton Abbott 5–0 and good play was reported from the wingers, Boultwood and Julian-Smith. The proceeds from the game went to the Urban Councils Fund for the Unemployed. In September, Plymouth Ladies travelled to St Austell to represent Devon against Cornwall. The first half ended 0–0 despite Plymouth's aggressive play and they dominated in the second half, winning 2–0. The gate numbered over 3,000.

The *WMN* published a fixtures list with matches organised throughout September and October plus other games planned against Bristol, Bournemouth, Weymouth, Yeovil, Torquay, Bideford, Ilfracombe and Tiverton. The report also detailed plans for the team's trip to France in late October to play in Paris and Havre. The British Ambassador, Lord Hardinge, was expected to attend and the team were looking forward to being presented to the French President and his wife. On 28 October there was a letter from 'A mother of a rejected member of the Plymouth team for the France trip', complaining that the inclusion of players from Cardiff, Swansea and Southampton was very unfair to the Plymouth girls who had trained conscientiously and remained loyal. Nevertheless, the team returned from France to an enthusiastic reception from friends and admirers. The girls had:

The time of their lives and were given a magnificent reception in both Paris and Havre. In their first game they were unlucky not to score a big victory with a 0-0 draw and the French press admitted they were the superior side. The replay in Havre was just as hotly contested and it was again a goalless draw. Several shots on goal from both sides were heroically saved.

But not all was positive. There had been much opposition to women's football and on 5 December 1921 the Football Association passed a unanimous resolution to block its progress, expressing its strong opinion that:

> The game of football is quite unsuitable for females and ought not to be encouraged.

FA clubs agreed to refuse the use of their grounds for women's matches. There was much support for the stance of the FA. In an article of 7 December 1921, the *WMN* quoted Dr Mary Scharlieb, a Harley Street Physician, who considered it: 'a most unsuitable game – too much for a woman's physical frame'. Mr Eustace Miles also felt that it was most inappropriate, especially if the women had not been medically tested first. He considered that kicking was too jerky and put severe strain on the body and that a woman's movements should be as rounded as her frame. He suggested cricket as a good game for women – but only as long as they did not throw the ball.

Women's football was quick to react. Quoted in the *WMN,* Mrs Boultwood, Captain of Plymouth Ladies said:

> The FA is one hundred years behind the times and their action is sex prejudice. None of the players had felt any ill effects from playing and actually felt healthier. Football was neither as fatiguing as swimming or as dangerous as hockey. They were determined to continue.

Mr Boultwood, the Hon. Secretary of the team, addressed the issue of charity payments, pointing out that over £1,000 had been distributed to charities all over the country and the loss of this income would be detrimental. The Ladies had a game against Southampton in a few weeks and he hoped that the arrangement would stand, although Plymouth Argyle had stated they had no choice but to accede to the FA request over use of their ground.

On 15 December 1921 the *WMN* reported that the action taken by the FA had only made the girls more determined. The English Ladies Football Association (ELFA) had been inaugurated and local leagues were being formed. Women's football was to be regularised and modifications would include a lighter ball. In early 1922 ELFA hosted its first league cup with the draw for the first round held on 18 February. Twenty-three teams had entered and Plymouth was drawn against Marazion. But this was a different team to the one which had travelled to France. The newly formed Plymouth and District Amateur Ladies Athletic and Football Club were entered into the league cup, while the original Plymouth Ladies became Plymouth International Ladies FC. There appears to have been some acrimony between the two teams and in the *WMN* of 20 December 1921 a series of letters to the editor show a split of support for the old team and the new. One even accuses the Internationals of having fielded a boy! One spectator wrote, having seen both teams play:

> If these are a fair sample of ladies' football I am of the opinion that it is not a game for women.

In a letter to the editor of 21 April 1922 the Chairman of Plymouth and District wrote to make it clear that there were two teams in Plymouth:

> One who can and do play good football and are in no way connected with the International team.

Earlier that year the International team again entertained the French but this match apparently owed more to fighting than football. One correspondent wrote to say that:

> Foul play was started by the French girls. The retaliation
> by the British girls was justified if perhaps unwise.

On 22 May 1922 the International Ladies beat Reading Ladies 7–1 before several thousand spectators, with Reading no match for the skill and combination of the Plymouth side.

In the ELFA cup, Plymouth and District beat Marazion in the first round on 27 March 1922. The game was played against a strong wind which made the lighter ball somewhat uncontrollable. The game ended 1–1, but the teams decided to play an extra twenty minutes with Plymouth scoring almost immediately for a final 2–1 victory. The team went through to the second round but were defeated by Ediswan. Stoke Ladies went on to win the one and only ELFA cup final. Although attempts were made to make the ELFA more commercial and a formal company was registered, it filed no accounts and the organisation quietly folded.

In the late 1960s the FA changed its view of the game 'being quite unsuitable for females', and in 1971 lifted the ban which stopped women playing on affiliated grounds. The Women's Football Association (WFA) formed in 1969 and within three years the first WFA Cup Final and England Women's international had been played. The exact date of the formation of the Plymouth Argyle Ladies team is not known but on 6 May 1976 the 'Plymouth Pilgrims' were officially registered with the WFA, the forerunner of today's team.

CHAPTER 18

Women and War

'Every fit woman can release a fit man...'

The First and Second World Wars had a significant impact on the role of women in society. During both conflicts, women were responsible for the 'Home Front' – required to take on jobs to free men for fighting and to help keep the country and war-machine functioning. New opportunities arose in the public, commercial and industrial sectors, and class, gender and social barriers were eroded. Women were tested and not found wanting, and their fortitude during the First World War laid the foundations for the emancipation which was to come. But as we shall see, once the wars ended, women were expected to return to their domestic roles.

The Call-Up

First World War conscription began with the passing of the Military Service Act on 2 March 1916. Initially single men between 18 and 41 were liable to be called up and not long after, this was extended to married men. Women had already begun to fill the roles left behind by men, despite initial resistance to women doing 'men's work', but with conscription the situation became urgent. The government coordinated the employment of women through campaigns, recruitment drives and numerous posters declaring 'every fit woman can release a fit man'. Women began to work in areas never before open to them – as railway guards and ticket collectors, bus and tram conductors, postal workers, police, etc., as well as jobs created specifically by the war such as in the munitions factories. Figure 18.1

Employment Sector	No. of Women Employed		Total Increase	Percentage Increase
	Jul 1914	Oct 1917		
Private Industry	2,176,000	2,706,000	530,000	24%
Government	2,000	216,000	214,000	10700%
Utilities	600	4,600	4,000	667%
Agriculture	80,000	89,000	9,000	11%
Transport	18,200	111,200	93,000	511%
Finance	9,500	67,500	58,000	611%
Commerce	496,000	831,000	335,000	68%
Professions	67,500	89,500	22,000	33%
Hospitality	176,000	200,000	24,000	14%
Post Office	60,500	107,000	46,500	77%
Other Civil Service	4,500	51,000	46,500	1033%
TOTAL	**3,090,800**	**4,472,800**	**1,382,000**	**45%**

Figures do not include domestic service, small workshops or women in naval, military or Red Cross hospitals

Fig. 18.1: Women's Employment Changes During First World War

shows the increase in the number of women in specific areas of employment.[1] Domestic service is not included but it was estimated that 400,000 domestic servants were displaced by the war, moving on to other occupations partly because of patriotic duty, but perhaps also as a release from the low-paid drudgery of such work.

At the outbreak of the Second World War the National Service (Armed Forces) Act was passed, which meant immediate conscription for all men aged 18 to 41. Women were again needed to fill the roles vacated by men, but it was clear that relying on the voluntary cooperation of women would not be enough this time. In December 1941 the National Services Act (No. 2) legalised the conscription of women who had the choice of entering the armed forces or working in farming or industry. Initially limited to single women aged 20 to 30 this was later expanded, and by mid-1943 it was estimated that ninety per cent of single women and eighty per cent of married women were involved in the war effort. Employment opportunities were broader than even in the First World War. Women drove and maintained vehicles, manned anti-aircraft guns and RADAR stations, ferried aircraft from factories to airfields, deciphered coded messages or worked as spies in the Special Operations Executive. By December 1943, one in three factory workers was female, building the tanks, guns and planes needed for the war. When war broke out in 1939 it was estimated that there were 5 million women in work; by 1943 the estimate was well in excess of 7 million.[2]

War Work in Plymouth

Plymouth did not have any major munitions factories but the dockyard provided many opportunities for women during both wars. Pay books held at the Devonport Naval Heritage Centre record the employment of women during the war years. For example, Miss A. James started work on 22 September 1916 at a rate of 18s. Her pay regularly increased until she was discharged on 22 February 1919 on a rate of 41s. Eight other women were employed on the same day and received similar pay increases. Reasons for the discharge of the women vary. Miss James was discharged by 'reduction', due to the return of men to the dockyard after the war. The *WMN* of 10 February 1919 reported that:

> A small number of women have received a fortnight's notice and further notices will be issued from week to week until all demobilised men have returned to their duties. The women are entitled to unemployment pay until they secure situations, up to the end of three months from the time they leave war work.

Other women requested to be discharged and two of the workers were suspended for insubordination, one for three days and the other for six. Both eventually requested to be discharged, one straight after the suspension and the second a few months later. Neither of these women received the same pay rises as others

Pay Book Entries for Female Dockyard Workers, First World War.
(Devonport Naval Heritage Centre)

Pay Book Entries for Female Dockyard Workers, First World War.
(Devonport Naval Heritage Centre)

employed at the same time and one cannot help but wonder if this was a reason for their insubordination, or whether their behaviour at work had already led to sanctions against them.

The Hurt Books at the Devonport Naval Heritage Centre record accidents and treatment. The records for the First World War do not always specify what jobs the women were doing but injuries such as contusions, lacerations, bruising and abrasions

Women Workers at the Dockyard, Second World War. (Devonport Naval Heritage Centre)

give a clear enough picture of women working as machinists, fitters and labourers. Two occupations which were singled out were an upholsteress who incised her left index finger, and a telephone operator who received a burn to her eyelashes – this last one is a little harder to picture!

The Hurt Books for the Second World War give more details. Women worked as electrical welders, cleaners, rivet girls, painters, drillers, and bench fitters. Some of the entries included:

- Eliza Crawley – contused wound of nose – stumbled during 'lights out' and struck nose heavily on floor of Erecting Shop.
- Florence Currie – contusion of left leg – struck against torpedo tube in torpedo tube shop.
- Edwards – contusion of scalp caused by iron bar falling on head working in ropery yard.

Women Workers at the Dockyard, Second World War. (Devonport Naval Heritage Centre)

- Beatrice Blackaller – electric shock from a live wire under repair near a water tap in dining room.
- Elizabeth Jewell – traumatic amputation of right index finger while working on revolving milling machine.

There were many other employment opportunities in Plymouth. Women were taken on as bus conductors and had four days training where they learned to make out report sheets, read fare and stage charts, check ticket books and deal with lost property. It took a short while to learn how to stand comfortably with the bus in motion, but usually by the end of the second day they had stopped falling about and could issue tickets and give change quite comfortably. The trainees were said to be delighted at the thought of receiving a wage-packet equal to the men (6*s* per day for eight hours work) and a week's holiday.

The *WMN* of June 1940 explained how Plymothians had taken kindly to the new bus conductors, and the girls said that travellers were helpful in every way. By July 1940 there were over 100 women working on the buses, issued with money bags and punches, alpaca uniforms with navy-blue peaked caps, a dust coat for the hot weather and a heavier overcoat. The *WMN* talked to some of the girls about what appealed to them. Rose Wood, 20, left a job as a waitress and another girl had worked in a dress factory in Manchester before coming to Plymouth. Both enjoyed the work as: 'there are always new faces, people are kind and time flies'. Many of the girls were earning higher wages than previously and were helping out at home with fathers and brothers away at war. One girl who was saving for her marriage was earning twice as much as she had been as a typist, as were three girls who had been working in laundry and domestic service. Most had doubled their peacetime earnings and also saved on wear and tear on clothing. The heaviest item on the clothes bill was said to be stockings, as one girl commented: 'one chance kick by a traveller and it's another pair gone to glory'.

Women land workers were also required during the First World War and a Woman's Land Service Corp (WLSC) was established at Saltash, with fifty members. However, according to the *WMN* of 8 July 1916, although notices were sent to local farms within a four-mile radius, there had only been one reply. Initially there was some hostility to women working on farms and one farmer dismissed two women workers after threats by workmen over pay. Members of the Saltash WLSC questioned why farmers appealed for their male workers to be exempt from conscription when there was competent women's labour left unutilised. But on reading the recruitment tribunals reported in the local papers, many farmers were appealing on behalf of their own sons and one can imagine the fear behind their actions.

A letter from Alfred Burden, the Hon. Secretary of the District War Agricultural Committee declared there should be no excuse that women could not do the work because of their 'delicate physical organisation'. The women were able and willing to do two-thirds of all the work necessary on a farm.

The Land Army of the Second World War was established in 1939 and at its peak in 1943 there were over 80,000 Land Girls undertaking farmwork such as ploughing, threshing, haymaking, lambing and more. The Timber Corps employed 6,000 alone, felling trees and running sawmills. The Land Army continued beyond 1945 due to post-war food shortages and was finally disbanded in 1950.

Voluntary Work

Voluntary work during both wars was a particularly important occupation for women with children and encompassed everything from knitting comforts for servicemen, to fundraising for Belgian refugees, to nursing. The *WMN* of 30 October 1915 reported that the Women's Aid in War Time working party at St Budeaux had just restarted after a short holiday and would meet weekly to organise and distribute tasks. They were currently working for the hospital supply department, making garments and sandbags and collecting new and second-hand clothing to be sent to the Belgians.

Voluntary Aid Detachments were set up by the Red Cross in 1909. Although open to both sexes, during the war far more women became involved. By mid-1914 the War Office announced that the total strength of VAD members across the country was 71,147, of which about two-thirds were women. The local papers reported that Devon was one of the leading counties with fifty-nine detachments, six of which were in Plymouth. In August 1914, the Plymouth headquarters of the British Red Cross Society announced they were open for all applications for enrolment. Those members possessing first aid and home nursing certificates would be used as efficiently as possible and all assistance was welcome whether financial, providing useful materials, or in making garments and bandages. Rest stations were to be set up at each landing stage and railway station where injured men might be brought in, stocked with medical comforts and in the charge of trained VAD nurses. By September it was reported that the Three Towns VADs had

Wartime Cookery, February 1919. (Western Morning News)

over 100 trained nurses and that this number would increase. The nurses in training gained valuable experience at military hospitals, the South Devon and East Cornwall and Royal Albert Hospitals and at the workhouse infirmary. In 1916, when experienced nurses began to be called up for military service,

Matron Harriet Hopkins at the SD & EC Hospital began to recruit VADs. Across the country there was apparently some animosity between the regular nurses and the VADs, who were often from the upper and middle classes and perceived to be in it just for the 'glamour' of nursing for the war effort. As the war progressed however, relations improved. Many VAD nurses served abroad and they were not immune from injury, disease and death – on 22 November 1915, the *WMN* reported the death of VAD nurse, Mrs H. Taylor who was a member of the Mediterranean Expeditionary Force. In 1917, a tented hospital of 200 beds was created on Millbay recreation ground, giving the VADs of Plymouth the opportunity to run a military hospital.

The main voluntary organisation of the Second World War was the Women's Voluntary Service, created in 1938 in the expectation of another major European conflict. Its original remit was for civil defence; to ensure women were prepared to deal with air attacks and protect themselves and others during hostile action. But as the war progressed the role expanded to include the organisation of evacuees, hospital supply services, making bandages and bedding, sewing and knitting for the men of the forces, manning first aid posts, ambulance driving, salvage collection and clerical work. By early 1939, under the leadership of the Marchioness of Reading, Stella Isaacs, there were 50,000 members, and by the late summer of that year membership stood at one third of a million and was still growing. One of the successes in recruitment was that the WVS was sensitive to the fact that women had families and commitments. They were only ever expected to give what time they could – even if that was only an hour a week.

The WVS was active in Plymouth and was up and running by August 1940. An information bureau was set up at 17 George Street and tasks included organising evacuations, sorting clothes donations, preparing registers of available accommodation for the homeless, aluminium collections, making up medical kits for ARP workers and rescue parties, knitting comforts and sorting and dispatching ration books.

In August 1941 the *WMN* reported that the Transport and General Workers Union Conference had demanded that women civil defence wardens were paid the same as men and would receive equal compensation for injury during air raids. In November 1941 the War Office sent an order to all Home Guard units that the training of women as unofficial units was not authorised, and that weapons and ammunition should not be used because women were not officially recognised as combatants. Dr Edith Summerskill MP questioned the decision, stating that women were already manning gun sites in the most dangerous situations and were prepared to take the risk. Despite the War Office order, in June 1942 the *WMN* reported that, when it was announced that men enrolled in the Civil Defence were to be trained by the Home Guard, women also took up the challenge. An enthusiastic squad of twenty women wardens were receiving unofficial hand-grenade and musketry training on two evenings a week. The best bomb-throwers were said to be able to hit targets at 20–30ft. On 26 April 1943, the *WMN* further reported that a group of around fifty women who were 'unofficial' members of the Home Guard had received training in drill, Morse code and signalling from a sergeant in the Royal Marines.

Plymouth's importance as a military base and dockyard made it a target for enemy action. In the summer of 1940 the first bombs were dropped, followed by the devastation of the Plymouth Blitz in 1941. On 20 and 21 March, huge swathes of the city were destroyed. The Royal Navy barracks was targeted and a petty officers' block destroyed, killing eighty. Seventy-two people were killed when an underground shelter in Portland Square suffered a direct hit. Four nurses, one mother and nineteen babies died after a hit on the Freedom Fields (City) Hospital. A further bombardment in April added to the destruction and left the death toll at 926.

Local WVS members worked with others sent in from outside Plymouth to deal with the shell-shocked survivors, setting up field kitchens and canteens to feed those now homeless. One member recalled:

Nancy Astor in the blitzed ruins of St Andrews Church. (South West Image Bank)

Margaret Smith, teacher at Plymouth High School for Girls had 'Resurgam' (I Will Rise Again) painted on a wooden board which she placed above the entrance to the ruined St Andrews Church. When the church was rebuilt the sign was carved in granite. (Chris Glasspool)

> Got out with canteen amid frightful rubbish, ruined homes, soldiers doing demolition ... nothing left of whole streets but twisted girders and rubble. People so pathetic, especially the kids.[3]

As well as the mobile kitchens, the WVS also supplied clothing for people left with only the tattered rags they had on. Another volunteer recalled:

> The clothing centre was a constant stream of white-faced weary women many with bandaged heads and limbs, of grimy unshaven men and crying puzzled children.[4]

In October 1941 Lady Reading made an appeal at Plymouth for more volunteers at a meeting at Central Hall which attracted an

The ruins of Charles Church. (Chris Glasspool)

audience of around 1,000 women. She praised the attitude and spirit of the city and advised women to:

> Get out and use your click-clacking tongues to spread the word. Not even Hitler's bombs can rob you of the power to be insistent as you talk.

The Regional Commissioner, Sir Hugh Elles, paid tribute to the work of women, saying that men had discovered the tremendous courage and endurance women possessed. In November there was a further appeal for more recruits to the Housewives Service

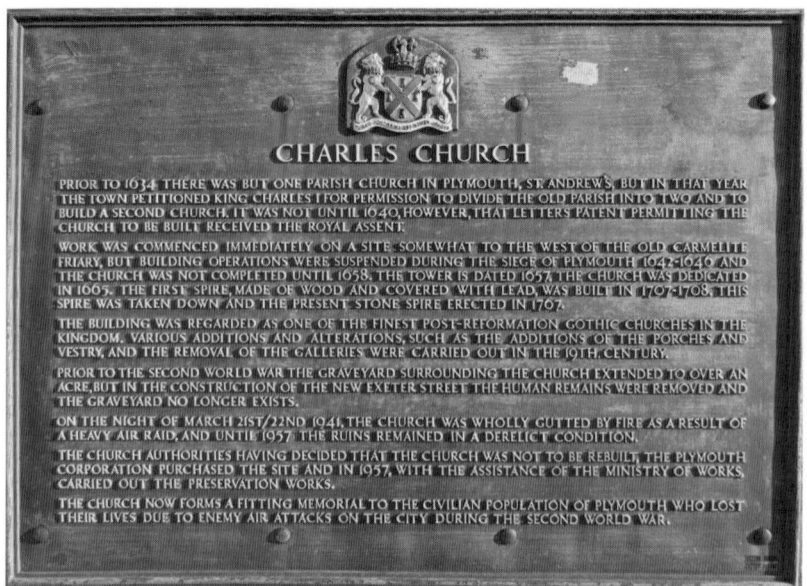

Blitz Memorial Plaque at Charles Church. (Chris Glasspool)

in Plymouth. Mrs Atkinson, technical advisor to the service, said that Plymouth had proved to her how capable women were but there was much for housewives still to do – helping wardens with information on occupants, offering shelter for casualties and domestic help in emergencies, salvage work and learning how to erect and operate emergency kitchens. The Housewives Service could be summed up by 'little acts of service, little periods of time given, little jobs well done'.

Other work included make-do-and-mend parties, fitting and repairing civilian gas masks and 'metal drives'. By March 1944 it was reported that Plymouth membership of the WVS stood at 5,792 including over 5,300 in the Housewives Section. In January 1945 they organised a collection called 'A Gift for London', as 'only those who had experienced the terrors of bombing could truly sympathise with those who were homeless'. In June 1945, Mrs Madeleine Alice Wordley, the County Borough organiser of Plymouth WVS, received an MBE. When war broke out she had been an ambulance team leader at a Plymouth First Aid Post before taking her role as borough organiser.

After the war the WVS carried on. In July 1949 the *WMN* reported that a fruit canning plant was open in the WVS Nissen hut. For a charge of sixpence, staff would 'can your fruit while you wait'. In September 1949 Lady Reading expressed thanks to all members of the WVS Plymouth who had made her so welcome on her recent visit. She was deeply impressed with the spirit of voluntary service and the wish to help the country.

Military Service

During both wars women were recruited into clerical and mechanical roles in the military services in order to free up men. On 13 August 1917 the *WMN* reported that approval had been given for the formation of the Women's Army Auxiliary Corps.

Occupations included clerks, librarians, accountants, typists, cooks, domestic staff, motor transport services, tailors, messengers, and

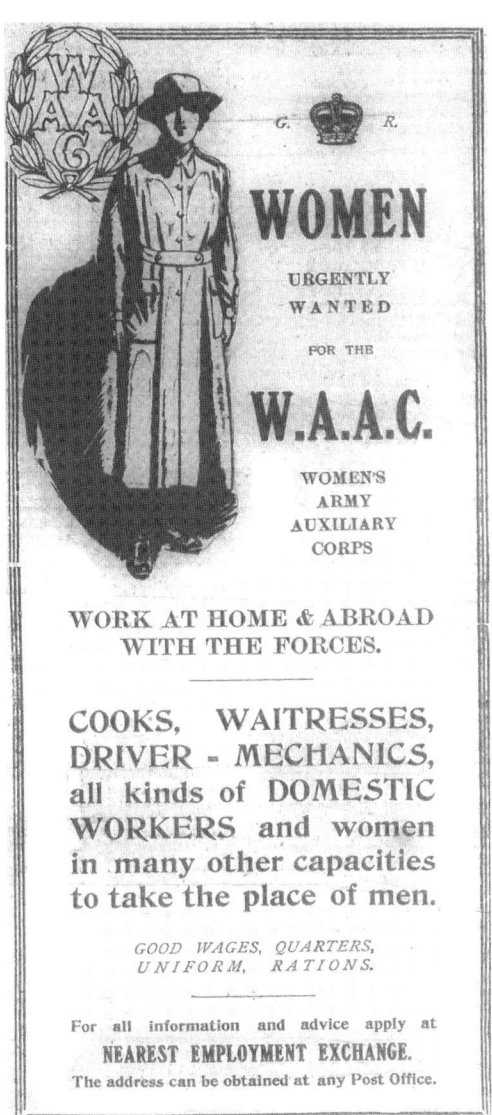

Recruiting for WAAC, September 1917. (Western Morning News)

telephone and postal services. All women serving overseas wore uniform, along with those at home who regularly entered barracks and camps. The minimum age was 18 for work at home and 20 for work overseas; those working away from home lived in hostels or billets.

Appointment was for one year or the duration of the war, and women were reminded that they were liable for arrest as deserters just as men were. The WAAC would not take women already employed in government departments, VAD workers, munitions workers, school teachers (unless given special permission) or matrons of workhouses. On 22 December 1917 the *WMN* reported on WAAC work in France noting that many of the 'damsels in khaki' had short hair. The newspaper wondered if this was to make them look more soldierly, but the reply was that 'in these dark cold mornings there is no time to do our hair properly'. Recruiters were keen to reassure parents that, in general, their daughters would be safe on joining the military services. However, there were casualties. On 11 June 1918 the *WMN* reported that between 15 May and 1 June, British hospitals in northern France had been bombed by the Germans on several occasions. The casualties were:

> Killed: 11 officers, 218 of other ranks, 5 Sisters, 8 WAACs, 6 civilians.
>
> Wounded: 18 officers, 634 of other ranks, 11 Sisters, 7 WAACs and 23 civilians.

In the Second World War, the WAAC reformed as the Auxiliary Territorial Service and by the end of the war had over 200,000 members. On 10 March 1939 the *WMN* reported that both general and local service companies of the ATS were being formed in Plymouth. Those in general service could be sent anywhere in the event of a national emergency; those in local service would stay in Plymouth. Mrs F Windeatt was the deputy commander of the local 41st Devon ATS, composed of cooks, orderlies, clerical workers and storewomen. The general service companies included the 9th Devon ATS for motor drivers and the 15th and 11th Devon ATS for clerical workers. On 15 June 1940 the Plymouth companies of the ATS marched through the streets of the city to bolster the enrolment of new recruits. At Millbay railway arch the salute was taken by the Senior Commandant, Miss K Acland, and in front of the Gaumont Palace Kinema the companies were inspected by Lady Astor, attended by Miss Acland and Company Commandant Miss G Faulkner. Inside the Kinema the women were cheered loudly as they took their seats and Lady Astor appealed urgently for recruits, and for women to give their time and service to their country.

On 14 September 1944 the *WMN* reported that a smiling ATS girl serving drinks on the platform was the first glimpse troops from Canada and the US had of British service-women. The girls gladly got up in the small hours to make insulators of tea and coffee and take them to the station when the message came through from command that a troop train was about to pass through. One such girl was Private Doris Hopper of Plymouth, who had been a laundry assistant before joining the ATS. In June 1945 Plymouth ATS member Kathleen Overbury went to Paris to help run the Army Exhibition which had just been opened by Field Marshal Montgomery and told the story of the British Army's contribution to victory in Europe. Private Overbury was in the anti-aircraft crews and was active in raids in Plymouth at the beginning of 1944.

The Women's Royal Naval Service formed in 1917 and by 1919 there were over 7,000 members, including cooks, stewards, despatch riders, sail makers and those working in intelligence. Their motto was 'Never at Sea'.

A contingent of WRNS at Devonport worked in various locations including on board ships at the dock and in barracks. On 15 April 1919 Dame Katherine Furze commenced a two-day inspection of the members and quarters of the WRNS stationed in the Plymouth Command. She was accompanied by the Divisional Director, Miss H Beale. She visited the Commander-in-Chief's offices where a number of WRNS were employed and went to the Naval telephone exchange. On the second day she visited RN barracks at Keyham and RMLI barracks at Stonehouse, both of which employed a number of WRNS. She also visited those members serving on establishments afloat.

WRNS First World War Memorial. (Chris Glasspool)

Many members of the military services were decorated and rewarded for their service during the war and on 10 May 1919 the *WMN* reported the following awards:

- Miss Helen Mary Beale, the Deputy Divisional Director of the WRNS was made an OBE. Miss Beale was in charge of the Devonport division, having taken up the post on 4 November 1918 to replace the previous Director Charlotte Noel who had transferred to the WRAF.
- Miss Olga Heather Franklin, daughter of Mr R. F. Franklin, secretary to the Admiral Superintendent of the Dockyard was made MBE. Miss Franklin was a Deputy Principal and senior WRNS officer at the Commander-in-Chief's office, Mount Wise, Devonport.
- Miss Annette Ina Crisp was made MBE. She was Deputy Principal in charge of members of the WRNS at the RN Barracks, Devonport, where she was stationed for twelve months.

WRNS Centenary 2017. (Chris Glasspool)

The WRNS re-formed during the Second World War and women were posted to every home and overseas unit – by 1945 there were 72,000 serving WRNS.

The range of employment saw women serving as radio operators, meteorologists, bomb range markers, and sea-going cipher officers and coders. In common with the other military services their roles were always non-combative. Plymouth WRNS again served at the Royal Naval Barracks and on training ships at Devonport. On 8 March 1940 Mrs Laughton Matthews, Director of WRNS, made a three-day inspection of the West Country and visited Devonport and Stonehouse. She was particularly impressed by the ability of the WRNS attached to the Royal Naval Barracks to learn drill and the *WMN* reported that she thought the march past smartly executed and would like to see the same wherever she inspected. She was delighted to hear such good reports from the naval officers and she thought learning drill made a big difference to improving discipline and morale – the women realised they were not just individuals but part of a service to which thousands belonged. Mrs Laughton Matthews also saw some of the WRNS shooting in the gallery and one petty officer scored twenty-eight points –

WRNS Second World War Memorial. (Chris Glasspool)

getting seven 'bulls' with seven shots. As in the First World War, service women were honoured for their work. On 3 January 1944 it was reported that Mrs E. V. Welby, commandant of the WRNS at Plymouth since 1939, had been awarded the CBE (military division) in the New Years Honours List.

Nurses served with the Queen Alexandra's Imperial Military Nursing Service, established in 1902 and the Territorial Forces Nursing Service formed in 1909 (renamed the Territorial Army Nursing Service in 1920), as well as with the VADs. Nurses served all over the world in difficult and dangerous situations. The *WMN* of 1 July 1944 reported that Sister N. Davies, a Plymouth member of the QAIMNS was a prisoner of war in Japan. In 1942 Sister Davies's mother had received notice from the Malayan government that her daughter had been one of over 100 civilians and military nurses evacuated from Singapore. Their small ship had then been heavily bombed and left sinking. The survivors, many wounded, were marooned for four days on the tiny island of Kebat without food and only two gallons of water between them. Sister Davies was reported to have done magnificent work both on the lifeboat and on the island, and the group were eventually rescued by a Chinese junk. She had been last reported at the Daboh Hospital on the island of Sinkep, still attending the wounded. British Army Casualty Lists held at the National Archives show three separate entries for Sister Davies. In May 1942 she is listed as 'Missing' in Malaya along with many other service men and women including three QAIMNS and a TANS nurse. In May 1944 she is listed as a prisoner of war in Japanese hands. Finally, in December 1945, she is listed as no longer being a prisoner of war. The casualty lists make for sobering reading. Of the four nurses initially reported as missing in Malaya along with Sister Davies, only one other survived. The other three women were either killed in action or died in the POW camps.

But life went on, and in April 1941 the *WMN* reported that a woman who had lost her bridal costume in a raid was married at Mutley Baptist Church, Plymouth in her ATS uniform. A guard of honour was formed by members of 'D' company of which the bride was section leader.

Warship Week

As part of the National Savings Campaigns of the Second World War, towns and cities were invited to hold Warship Weeks with the aim of raising enough money to pay for the building of a particular ship which was then adopted by that town. In March 1942 the *WMN* announced that Plymouth's campaign would open on 21 March 1942, the anniversary of the first Blitz on the city. A target of £1,200,000 was set and fundraising included concerts, football matches and dances. As an extra push, Portsmouth was holding its Warship Week at the same time and there was friendly and spirited rivalry between the two. Lady Astor called on Plymouth women to help build more ships and

No. 213/1673.

H.M.S. ADVENTURE,
c/o G.P.O.,
LONDON.
2nd March, 1942.

Sir,—

It is with great pleasure I learn that H.M.S. Adventure has been adopted unanimously as the choice of Plymouth for the forthcoming Warship Week.

The ship, as you are aware, was built and completed in Devonport Dockyard, and we all appreciate the sterling work which was put into her.

It may be of interest to recall that this is the sixteenth ship of the Royal Navy to bear the name of Adventure, the first one dating from 1594; and that the Ship's Badge, taken from the Adventure Model of 1650, consists of "an anchor silver between two shields bearing the Cross of St. George and the Irish Harp." and the Ship's Motto is: "Dare All."

I have been asked by the Ship's Company to forward a cheque for £30 from the Ship's Fund to purchase War Savings Certificates for the benefit of the Trafalgar Orphan Homes; I am sending this through you as a contribution to be included in the Plymouth Warship Week.

On behalf of all those serving in H.M.S. Adventure, I wish all possible success to the Plymouth Warship Week.

I have the honour to be,
Sir,
Your obedient servant,
(sd.) N. V. GRACE,
CAPTAIN.

PLYMOUTH WARSHIP WEEK

MARCH 21 — 28th, 1942

OBJECTIVE £1,200,000

Issued by the Plymouth Warship Week Committee.

Plymouth Warship Week, March 1942. (Western Morning News)

26 March 1942 was designated 'Ladies Day', with the whole of the takings for the day credited to the women of Plymouth. The march past included detachments of the WRNS, ATS, WAAF, Women in Civil Defence, Nursing, Ambulance Service, WVS and NAAFI. Lady Astor took the salute and in a speech said:

> Ladies Day was the first of its kind in Plymouth. Men watched with admiration, surprise and some almost

with fear when they see their women-kind marching to the drum. On the whole I believe it is mostly admiration.

Nancy Astor used the moment to highlight the importance of the work women were doing in the war and that brains and ability were not the privilege of just one sex. She later visited the exhibition tent and inscribed a message on a bomb – 'One from Lady Astor'. On 1 April 1942 it was announced that Plymouth had raised an incredible £1,430,135 and they had not only exceeded their target, but also beaten Portsmouth by nearly £150,000.

After the War

At the end of the First World War there were an estimated one and a half million women directly replacing men in industry. As munitions factories closed or moved back to peacetime work, and men began to return home after demobilisation, there was huge pressure from the press, government committees and trade unions for women to give up their jobs for the sake of the returned men.

In 1919 the *WMN* reported on the inaugural meeting of the Comrades of the Great War and the National Federation of Discharged Soldiers and Sailors held in Plymouth. The meeting proposed a number of resolutions to be put forward to the prime minister and the Admiralty concerning the WRNS including that:

LADIES' DAY TODAY

PLYMOUTH WARSHIP WEEK

GRAND PARADE including W.R.N.S., A.T.S., W.A.A.F.s, W.V.S., Nurses, V.A.D. Salute to be taken by Lady Astor, 2.45 p.m. The whole of the day's takings to be credited to the Ladies of Plymouth

SPECIAL WARSHIP WEEK BALL at The Guildhall, 7.30 — 11 p.m.

By kind permission of the Commanding Officer

The Pipers of an Irish Regiment will be on the Hoe from 6.30 p.m. TODAY, FRIDAY, & SATURDAY

Plymouth Warship Week – Ladies Day March 1942. (Western Morning News)

Collecting for Warship Week, March 1942. (South West Image Bank)

> In view of the large number of ex-officers and men
> unemployed, the re-employment of officers and ratings
> of the WRNS in a civilian capacity in government
> establishments be prohibited and the Admiralty be
> requested to fill such positions with ex-service men.

There was some controversy over the employment of female
tram inspectors in Plymouth even before the war had ended.
Minutes of the Plymouth Council Tramways Committee
meeting of 17 June 1918 record that five women had been
employed as inspectors to fill vacancies caused by military
service call-up, but there was much opposition, with letters to
the newspapers suggesting that discharged servicemen should be
employed instead. Organisations such as the Comrades of the
Great War frequently sent letters of protest, but the Tramways
Committee maintained that in making appointments they had
never overlooked the claims of discharged servicemen and that
employment had been given to no less than fifty-nine such men.

The appointment of women inspectors was made at the suggestion of the National Service Authorities to enable discharged men to undertake more important work in the national interests. A letter of 12 July 1918 in the *WMN* from 'Justice', described the employed women as, 'those mean enough to deprive their late protectors of their rightful reward', and called on the need to break down the 'woman barrier which is a growing menace to the employment of men'. Other groups joined in the protest, including the National Union of Railwaymen and the Amalgamated Society of Tailors and Tailoresses. Even the Plymouth Tramway employees themselves protested against the statement made by the chairman of the Tramways Committee that there was no friction in the staff over the employment of female inspectors and that in fact the question was causing them grave concern. This was obviously an emotive subject and it shows the depth of feeling there was about women taking men's work, particularly those that had been fighting for their country. But it also leads one to wonder over the circumstances of the women employed. Were they widows or wives of injured soldiers, did they have dependants and a need to provide for families just as much as the discharged servicemen?

In 1918 a conference on the Position of Women in Industry after the War was convened by the Bristol Association for Industrial Reconstruction. It recognised that while some women would be happy to return to their pre-war lives, an unknown number would want to remain in industry. Others would need to earn their own living to support male relations who had been incapacitated by the war, and others would need to do so simply because their menfolk would not return. It was agreed that women should, as a matter of course, relinquish those jobs in which they had replaced men, directly or indirectly attributable to the war. The conference also raised the old issue which had dogged women throughout the decades – that of the belief that a woman's place was in the home. This was given added weight due to concerns over the health of the nation following the war. Responsibility for the country's future survival was laid at the feet of women, who needed to produce strong and stable families. The conclusion was that:

> Women should only be employed as factors in industrial efficiency in so far as the interests of family life and healthy development of the race are not prejudiced.

One solution mooted was to encourage women to return to the domestic service roles that they had left in their thousands during the war. It was at least recognised that conditions of work, holidays and wages would need to be improved, but those who wanted domestic servants were often reluctant to do so. Although many women did return to service, no doubt due to lack of other opportunities, these tended to be older women and the First World War sounded the death knell for domestic service. Women had sampled more rewarding, better paid work with more personal freedoms. By 1931 the number of women employed in domestic service had fallen to eight per cent of the female population from a high of thirteen per cent pre-war.[5]

In 1919 the government passed the Restoration of Pre-War Practices Act with the aim of forcing women to leave their wartime roles. The Bill was first debated in Parliament in July 1919 with some opponents deploring its brutal methods, which not only prevented women from taking part in the industries they had largely created, but also made it a criminal offence to employ them. An amendment was moved to soften the Bill but this was defeated. It has been estimated that in 1920 there were a million fewer women working than there had been at the height of the war years.[6] For those that did remain in work, their wages often did not remain at their wartime high, and studies have shown that by 1931 a working woman's weekly wage had returned to the pre-war situation of being half that of the male rate in most industries.[7]

The situation after the Second World War was more complex. There was again the assumption that women would make way for the returning troops, having only temporarily been doing a 'man's job', but in 1947 an economic survey showed that the labour force fell short of that required and women were encouraged to enter industry if they were in a position to do so.[8] The number of women remaining in work was higher than after the First World War but wages remained lower than men's, wartime nurseries closed, leaving women with childcare issues, and the idea remained that respectable wives and mothers did not work.

But the number of women who remained working was only one aspect. Perhaps the most important legacy of both wars was the change in consciousness as to what could and should be possible for women, and the breaking of many of the social, economic and political barriers that had existed. New, if temporary, opportunities gave women freedoms they had previously lacked, released them from the restrictions of domestic service and gave them money to spend which they had never had before. Many left home to live in hostels and lodging houses with their peers, rather than a more protected existence at home. Thousands of middle-class women who volunteered for the war effort also found their lives transformed. Freed from their cloistered existence they were expected to work and look after themselves with many experiencing war directly at the frontlines. The First World War hastened the collapse of traditional women's employment such as domestic service and was swiftly followed by the passing of the Representation of the People Act in 1918, and the Sex Disqualification (Removals) Act in 1919. Even if life did slip back to pre-war standards, the Second World War again showed women what they could achieve. Policy makers began to agree that women could combine work, marriage and motherhood, and a Report of the Royal Commission on Population published in 1949 acknowledged that women could do two jobs and there was 'nothing inherently wrong in the use of mechanical means of contraception'.[9] Women were more aware of their potential and this laid the groundwork which led directly to the fight against gender inequality and increased feminist activity of the 1960s and 70s.

References

Chapter 1: The Changing Role of Women

1.   Goodall, F. (2009) *Lost Plymouth.* Birlinn Ltd, Edinburgh.

Chapter 2: Prostitution and Protest: Plymouth and the Contagious Diseases Acts

1.   Goodall, F. (2009) *Lost Plymouth.* Birlinn Ltd, Edinburgh.

2-4.   Walkowitz, J.R. (1980) *Prostitution and Victorian Society: Women Class and the State.* Cambridge University Press, Cambridge.

5.   Goodall, F. (2009) *Lost Plymouth.* Birlinn Ltd, Edinburgh.

6.   McDonald, L. (Ed) (2012) *Florence Nightingale and Hospital Reform: Collected Works of Florence Nightingale Vol. 16.* Wilfrid Laurier Univ. Press, Ontario.

7-10.   Walkowitz, J.R. (1980) *Prostitution and Victorian Society: Women Class and the State.* Cambridge University Press, Cambridge.

Chapter 3: Educating Girls

1.   *The Life of a Girl in the United Services Orphanage 1907–1916,* Plymouth and West Devon Record Office 571.

2.   www.educationengland.org.uk

3.   Plymouth & West Devon Record Office 1644/1-9.

Chapter 4: Doctors and Nurses

1.   www.memoriesofnursing.co.uk

2.   PWDRO 1228/182.

Chapter 6: Maternity and Childbirth

1. Davies, M.L. (1978) *Maternity: Letters From Working Women.* Virago, London.

2. Lewis, J. (1984) *Women in England 1870–1950.* Harvester Wheatsheaf, Hemel Hempstead.

3. Spring Rice, M. (1981) *Working-Class Wives.* Virago, London.

4-5. Lewis, J. (1984) *Women in England 1870–1950.* Harvester Wheatsheaf, Hemel Hempstead.

Chapter 7: Plymouth in Profile: The Battle for Birth Control

1. Lewis, J. (1984) *Women in England 1870–1950.* Harvester Wheatsheaf, Hemel Hempstead.

2. www.fpa.org.uk/factsheets/history-family-planning-services

3. Simms, M. 'History of Contraceptive Care' in *Journal of the Royal College of General Practitioners*, February 1978.

4. Lewis, J. (1984) *Women in England 1870–1950.* Harvester Wheatsheaf, Hemel Hempstead.

Chapter 8: Marriage and the Home

1. Lewis, J. (1984) *Women in England 1870–1950.* Harvester Wheatsheaf, Hemel Hempstead.

2. Lewis, J. (1984) *Women in England 1870–1950.* Harvester Wheatsheaf, Hemel Hempstead.

3. Van Der Kiste, J. (2009) *History and Guide: Plymouth.* The History Press, Stroud

4. Van Der Kiste, J. (2009) *History and Guide: Plymouth.* The History Press, Stroud

5. www.wes.org.uk/content/electrical-association-women

6. Lewis, J. (1984) *Women in England 1870–1950.* Harvester Wheatsheaf, Hemel Hempstead.

Chapter 9: Poverty & Philanthropy

1. Higginbotham, P. *The Workhouse,* www.workhouses.org.uk

2. Williams, T.J. (1965) *Priscilla Lydia Sellon.* Richard Clay (The Chaucer Press), London.

3-4. www.anglicanhistory.org/bios/plsellon.html

Chapter 10: Women in Profile: Dame Agnes Weston

1-2. Weston, A. (1913) *My Life Among the Bluejackets.* James Nisbet & Co., Plymouth.

3. www.aggies.org.uk/about-aggie

Chapter 11: Votes for Women

1. http://www.parliament.uk/documents/parliamentary-archiv es/1866SuffragePetitionNamesWebJune16.pdf

2. www.hansard.millbanksystems.com

3. Rendell, M. (2008) *The Campaign in Devon For Women's Suffrage.* In Transactions of the Devonshire Association, No.140.

4. Liddington, J. Crawford, E. (2011) 'Women Do Not Count, Neither Shall They Be Counted'. In *History Workshop Journal*, Vol 71, Issue 1, March 2011.

5. Goodall, F. (2009) *Lost Plymouth.* Birlinn Ltd, Edinburgh.

Chapter 12: Jobs for the Girls

1. Ryan, J (2011) *Women Naval Dockyard Workers in Two 19th Century Dockyard Towns: Chatham and Plymouth.* Thesis submitted to University of Greenwich.

2. bbc.co.uk/history/british/Victorians

3-6. Ryan, J (2011) *Women Naval Dockyard Workers in Two 19th Century Dockyard Towns: Chatham and Plymouth.* Thesis submitted to University of Greenwich.

7.   www.bbc.co.uk/history/british/Victorians

8.   Lewis, J. (1984) *Women in England 1870–1950*. Harvester Wheatsheaf, Hemel Hempstead.

9.   Pointon, V.F.T (1989) *Mid-Victorian Plymouth: A Social Geography*. PhD Thesis, Polytechnic South West.

10-11. www.olddevonport.uk

12.   www.first100years.org.uk

Chapter 14: Public and Community Life

1.   www.historyofwomen.org

Chapter 15: Women in Profile: Nancy Astor

1-2. www.hansard.millbanksystems.com

Chapter 18: Women and War

1.   From A *Conference on the Position of Women in Industry after the War* convened by the Bristol Association for Industrial Reconstruction. PWDRO 186/11/11.

2.   www.bbc.co.uk/guides/z2j9d2p

3-4. Malcolmson, R. and P. (2013) *Women at the Ready: The Remarkable Story of the Women's Voluntary Services on the Home Front*. Little, Brown, London.

5.   www.bbc.co.uk/history/british/britain_wwone/women_employment

6.   www.socialistreview.org.uk/400/women-and-first-world-war

7.   www.bbc.co.uk/history/british/britain_wwone/women_employment

8.   Lewis, J. (1984) *Women in England 1870–1950*. Harvester Wheatsheaf, Hemel Hempstead.

9.   Lewis, J. (1984) *Women in England 1870–1950*. Harvester Wheatsheaf, Hemel Hempstead.

Bibliography

Davies, M.L. (1978) *Maternity: Letters From Working Women.* Virago, London.

Goodall, F. (2009) *Lost Plymouth.* Birlinn Ltd, Edinburgh.

Gray, T. (2009) *Remarkable Women of Devon.* Mint Press, Exeter.

Lewis, J. (1984) *Women in England 1870-1950.* Harvester Wheatsheaf, Hemel Hempstead.

Malcolmson, R. and P. (2013) *Women at the Ready: The Remarkable Story of the Women's Voluntary Services on the Home Front.* Little, Brown, London.

McDonald, L. (Ed) (2012) *Florence Nightingale and Hospital Reform: Collected Works of Florence Nightingale Vol. 16.* Wilfrid Laurier Univ. Press, Ontario.

Pankhurst, E. (1913) *My Own Story.* Eveleigh Nash, London.

Purvis, J. (2000) *Women's History: Britain, 1850-1945.* Routledge, London.

Rendell, M. (2008) *The Campaign in Devon for Women's Suffrage.* In Transactions of the Devonshire Association, No.140.

Spring Rice, M. (1981) *Working-Class Wives.* Virago, London.

Van Der Kiste, J. (2009) *History and Guide: Plymouth.* The History Press, Stroud.

Walkowitz, J.R. (1980) *Prostitution and Victorian Society: Women Class and the State.* Cambridge University Press, Cambridge.

Weston, A. (1913) *My Life Among the Bluejackets.* James Nisbet & Co., Plymouth.

Williams, T.J. (1965) *Priscilla Lydia Sellon.* Richard Clay (The Chaucer Press), London.

Websites

www.aggies.org.uk
www.anglicanhistory.org
www.bbc.co.uk/history
www.bmj.com
www.childrenshomes.org.uk
www.donmouth.co.uk
www.educationengland.org.uk
www.first100years.org.uk
www.fpa.org.uk
www.hansard.millbanksystems.com
www.herstoria.com
www.historyextra.com
www.historylearningsite.co.uk
www.historyofwomen.org
www.histpop.org
www.localhistories.org
www.memoriesofnursing.uk
www.oldplymouth.uk
www.parliament.uk
www.qaranc.co.uk
www.scarletfinders.co.uk
www.socialistreview.org.uk
www.spartacus-educational.com
www.thehistorypress.co.uk
www.wes.org.uk
www.workhouses.org.uk

Index